Olga Goloveshkina

Stress Relief Coloring Book: Adult Coloring

Horse and Architecture

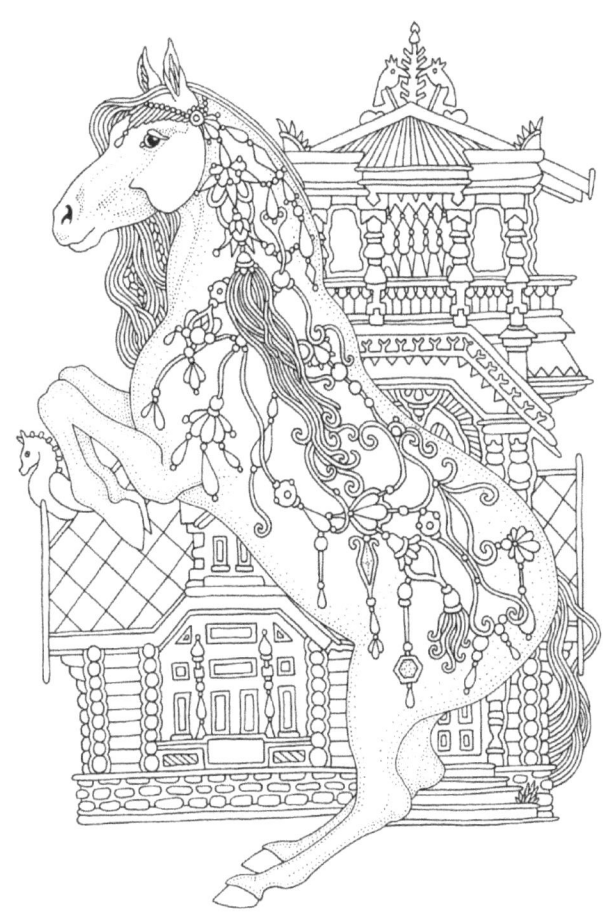

Olya's SketchBook 2

ISBN:1540676595
ISBN-13:9781540676597

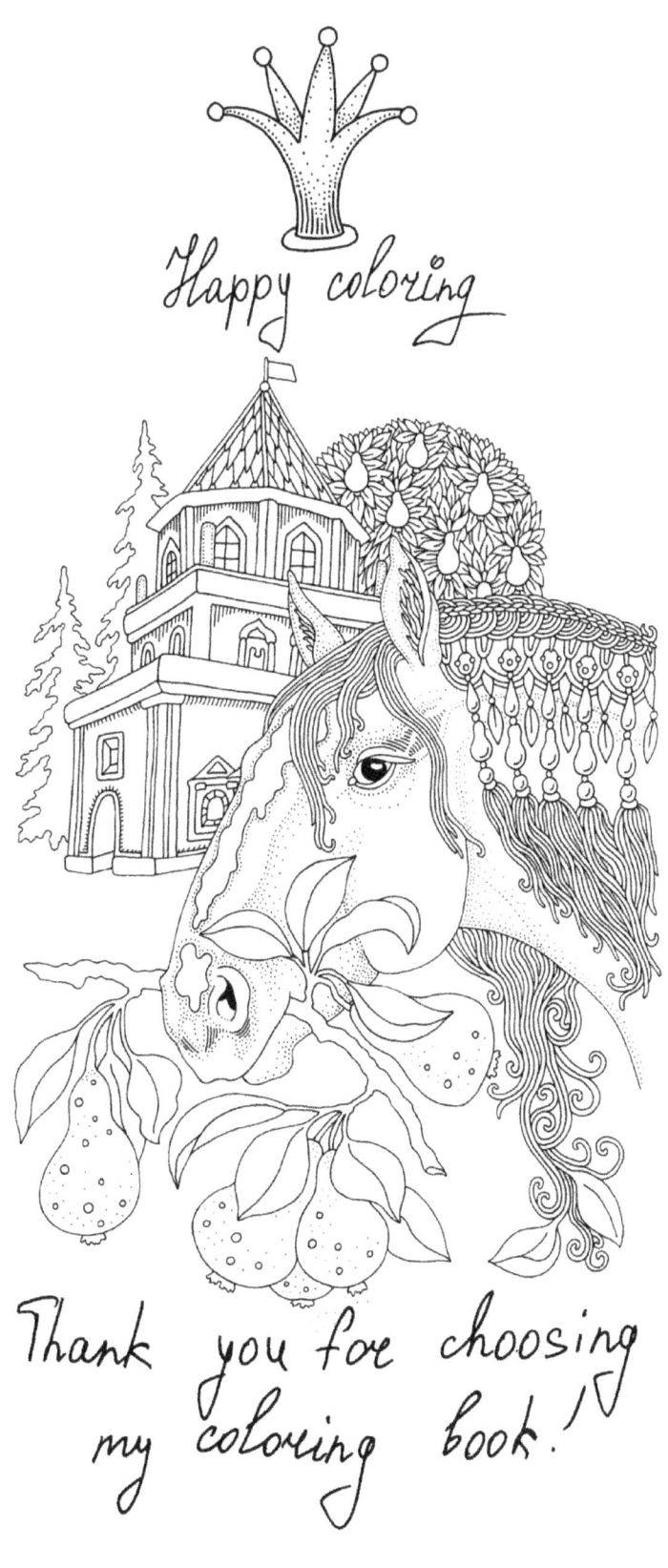

Happy coloring

Thank you for choosing
my coloring book!

Olya :)

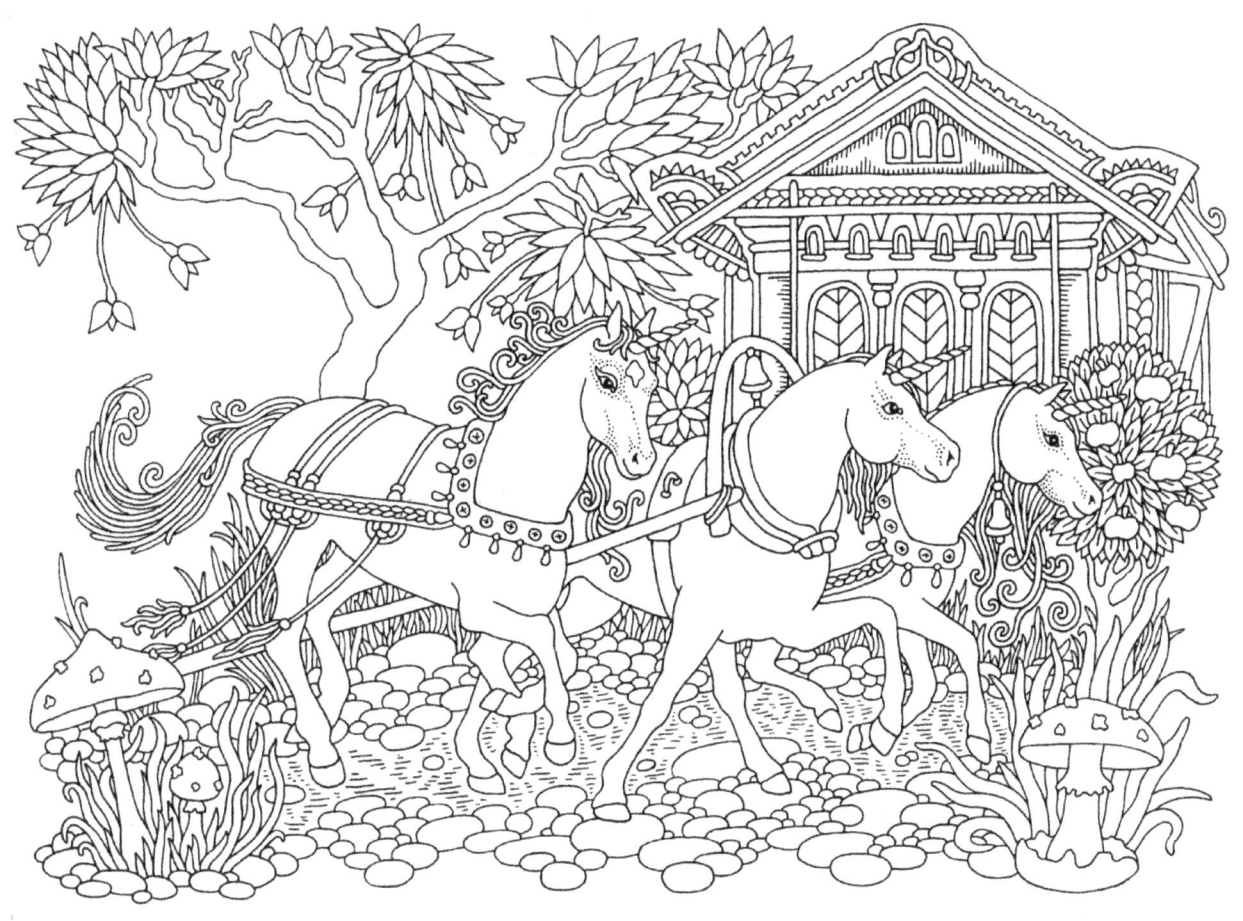

This book belongs to

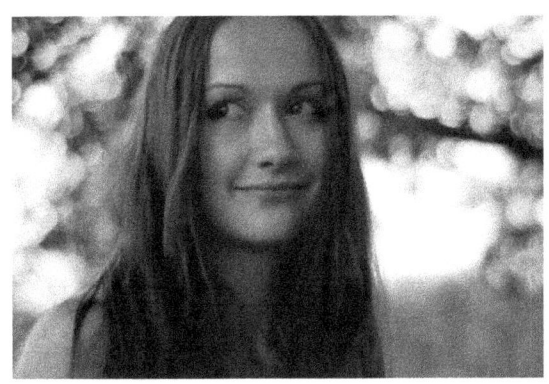

ABOUT THE AUTHOR

Olga Goloveshkina is a freelance artist and illustrator
based in Moscow, Russia.
She graduated from the Institute of Business and Design.
Olga specializes in black ink doodles.
She is an author and illustrator coloring books for adults
"The wind carries flowers"/"Veter unosit tsvety" (in Russian),
"Fox travel: Coloring book", "Mounts: Coloring book" (in English).

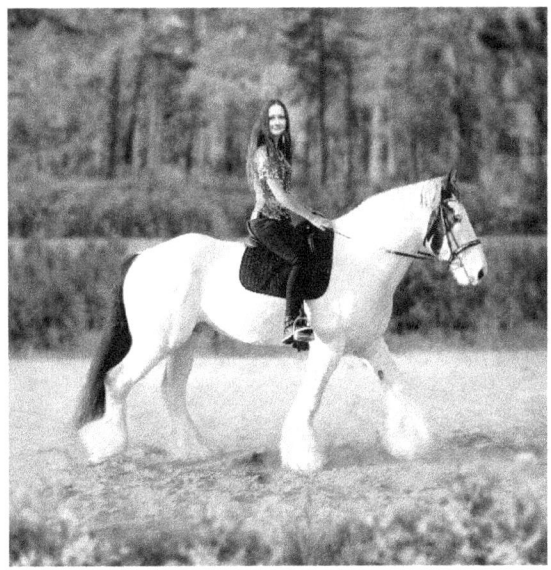

Author page on Amazon:

amazon.com/author/olgagoloveshkina

Site: http://olyagoloveshkina.jimdo.com

Instagram:

@olyahitrayapanda

@olyagoloveshkina

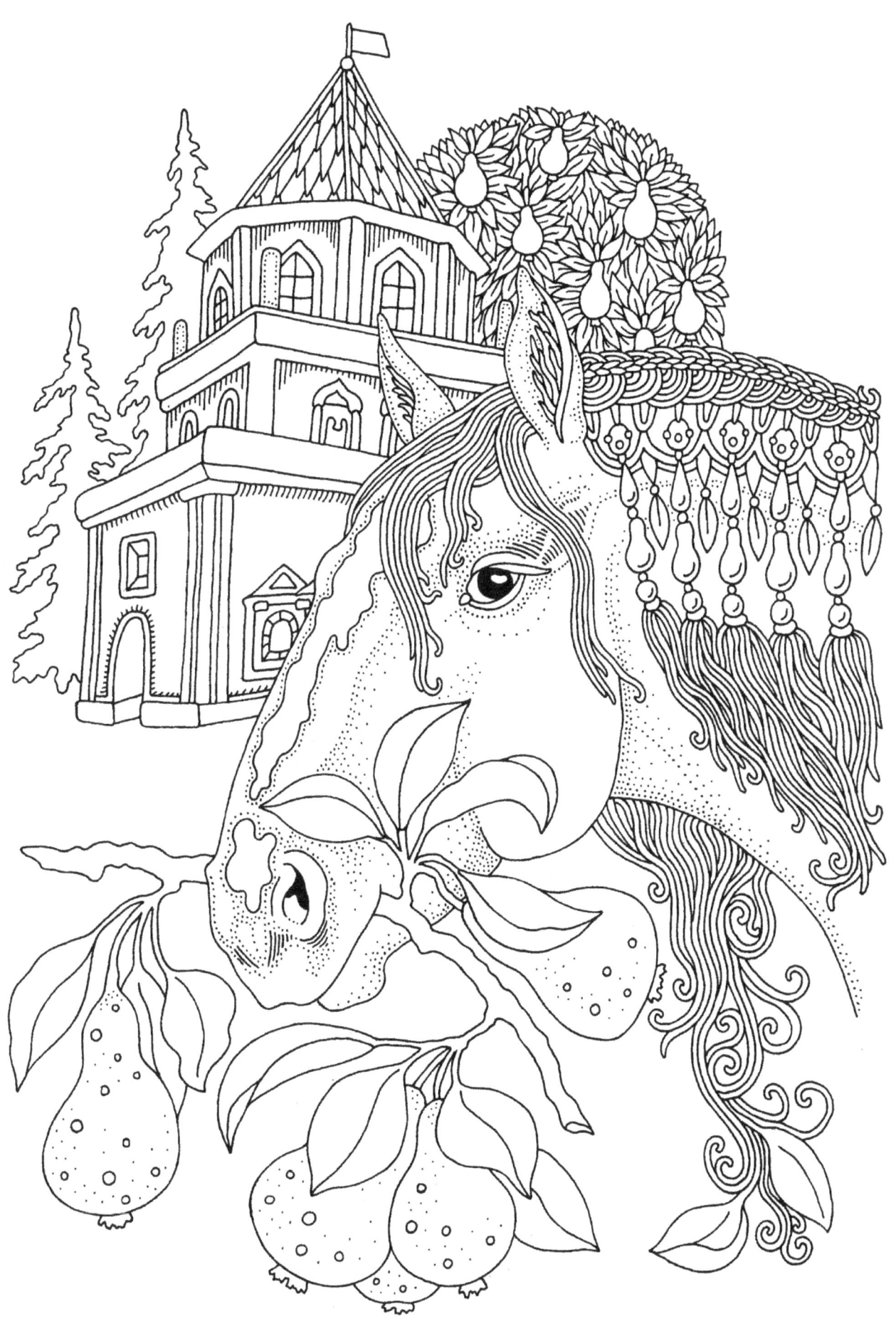

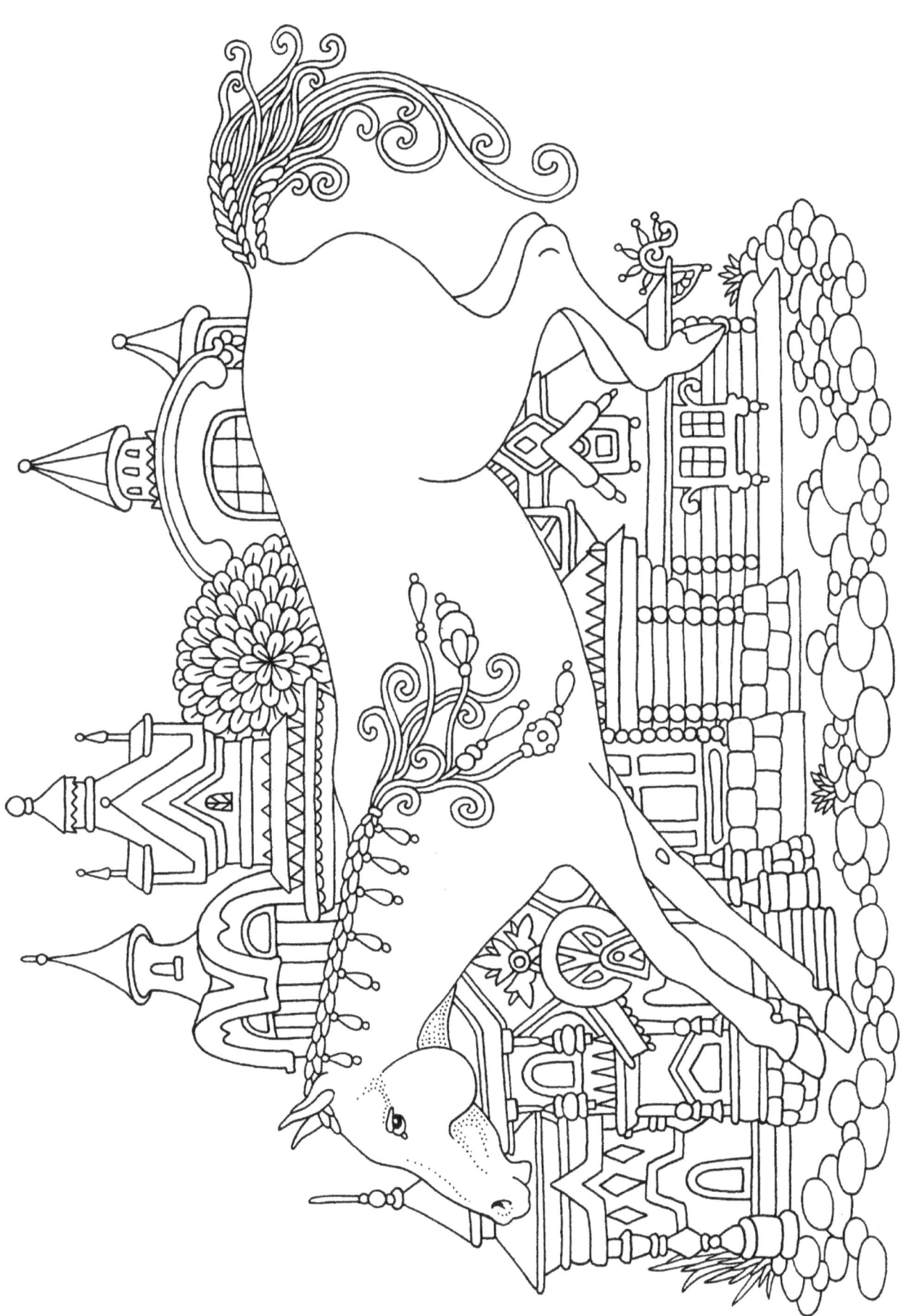

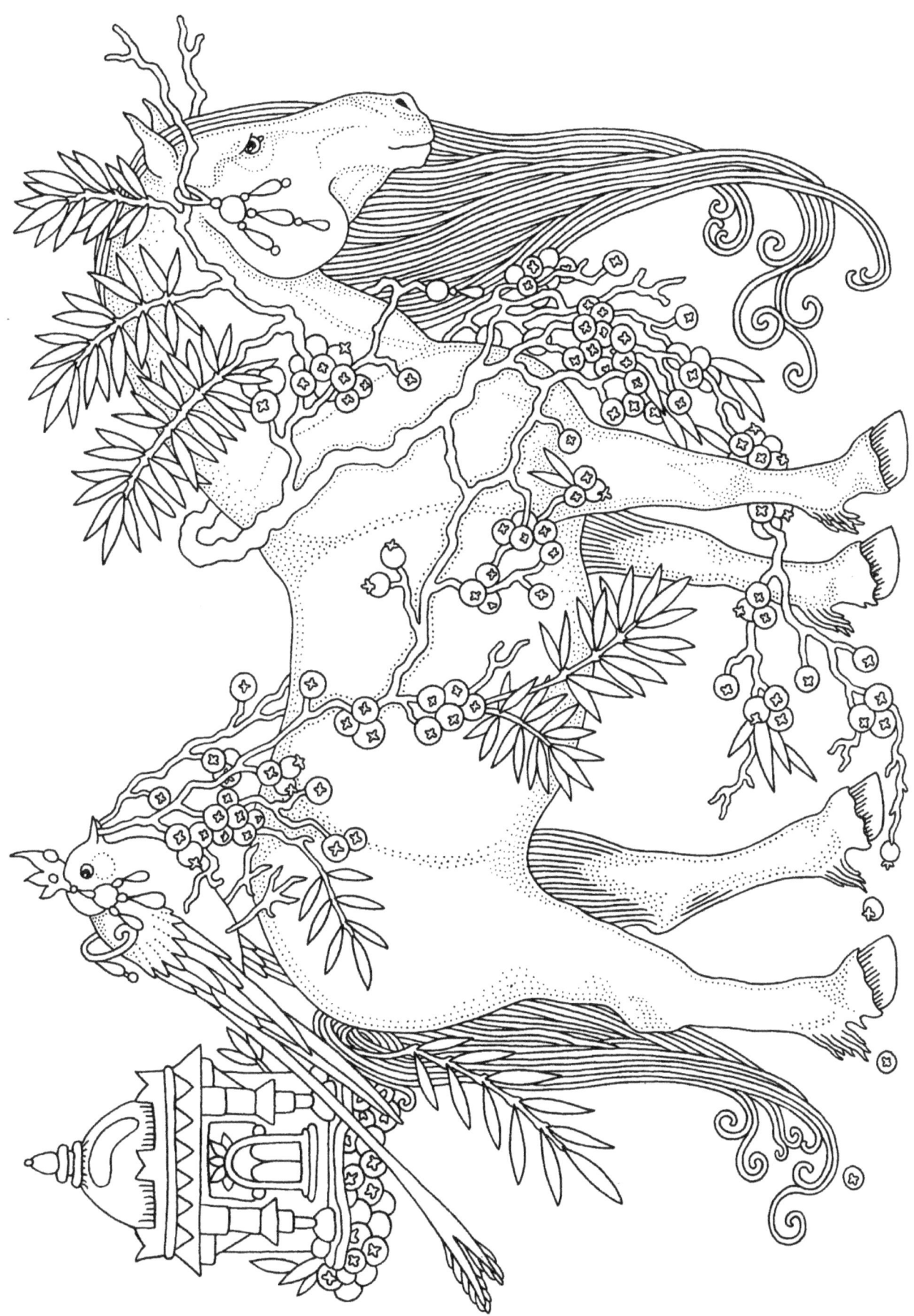

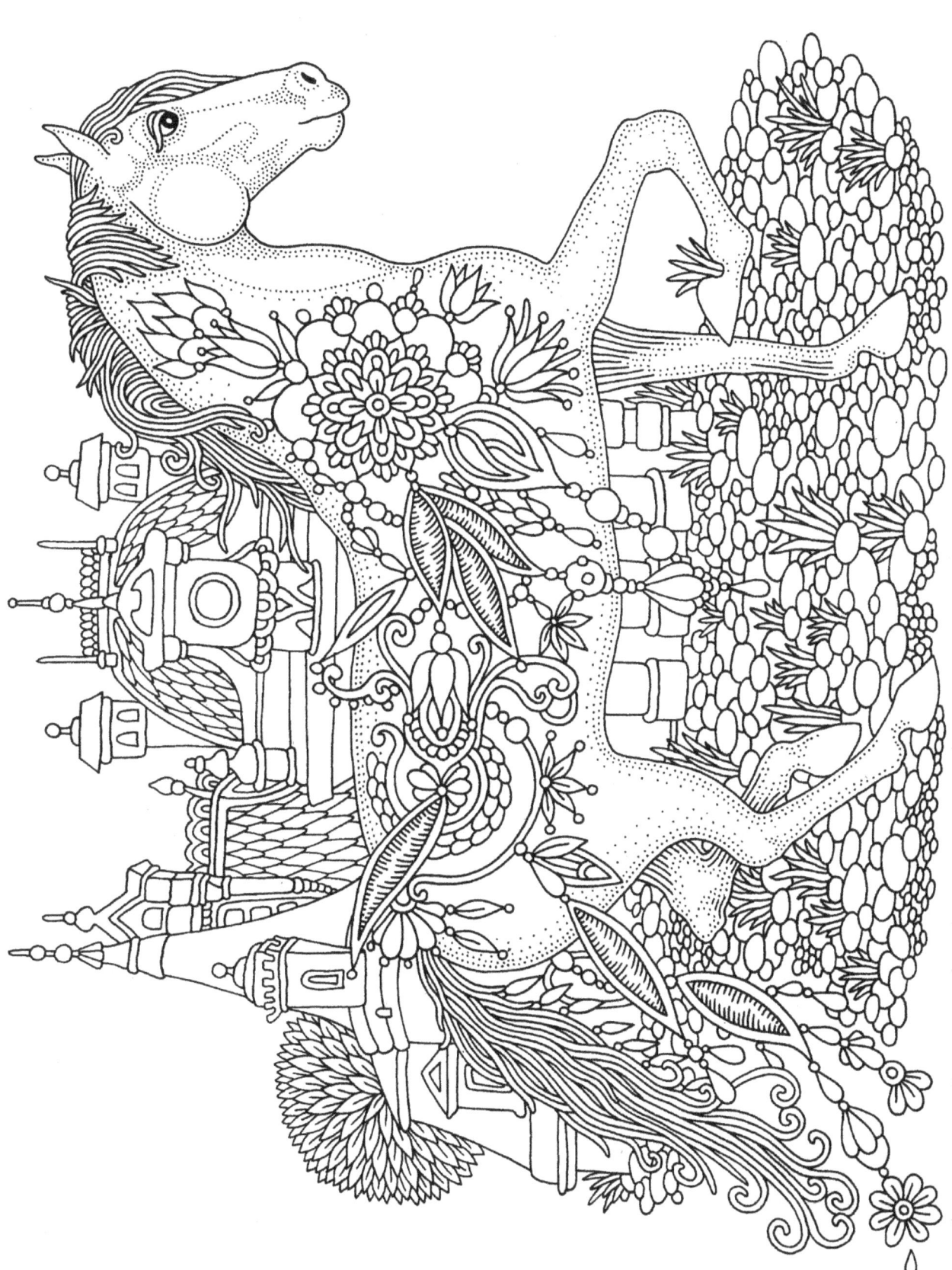

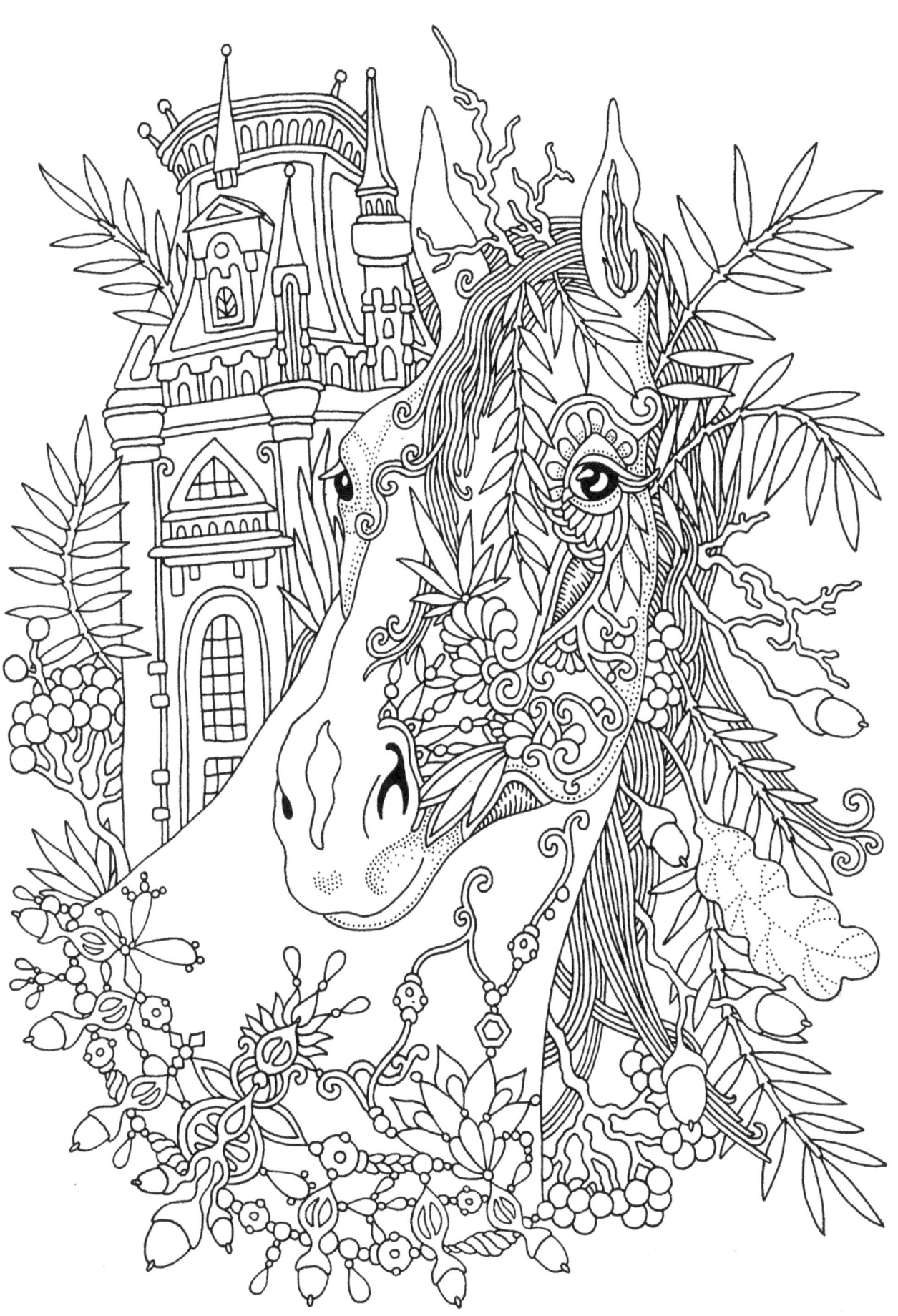

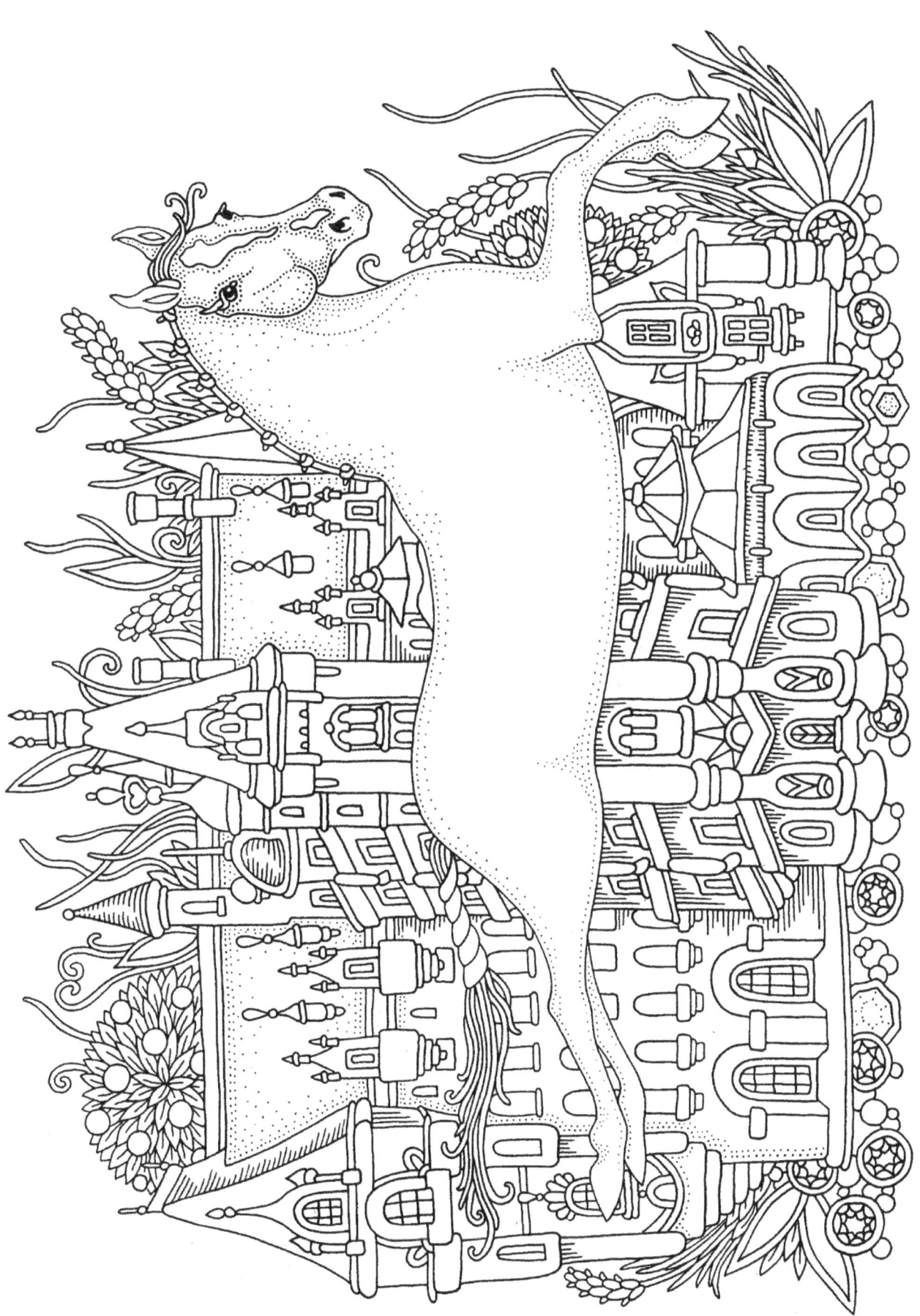

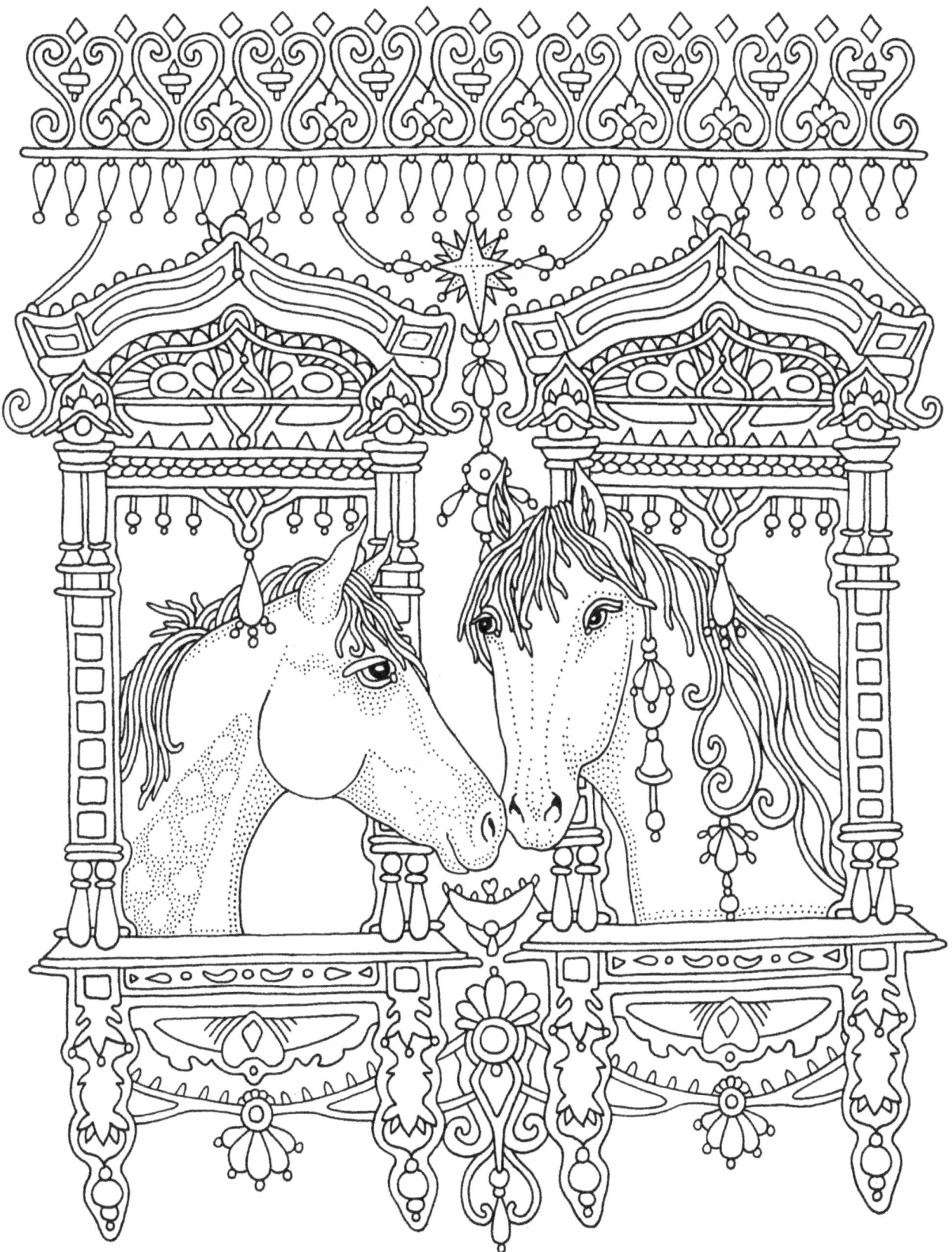

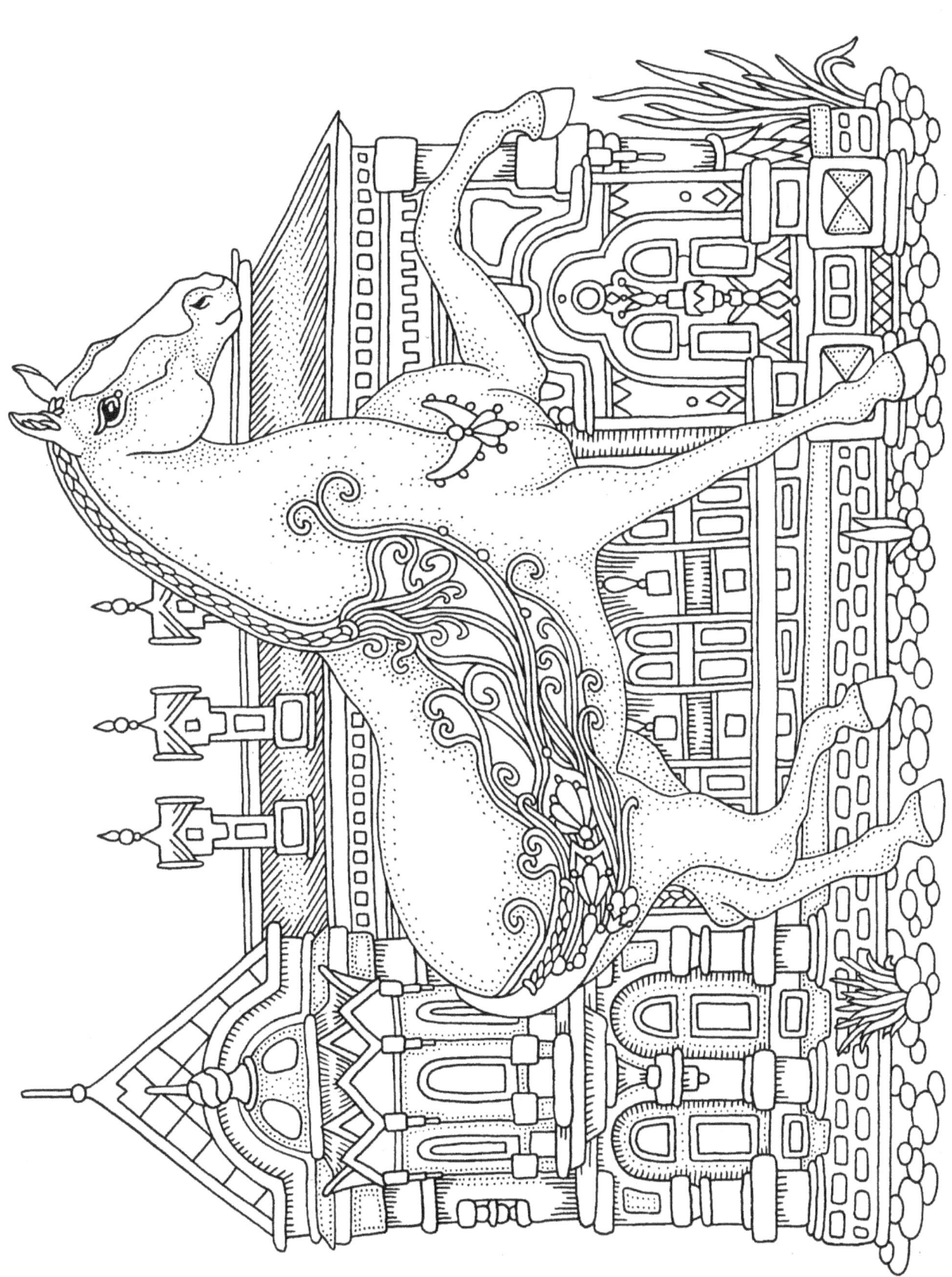

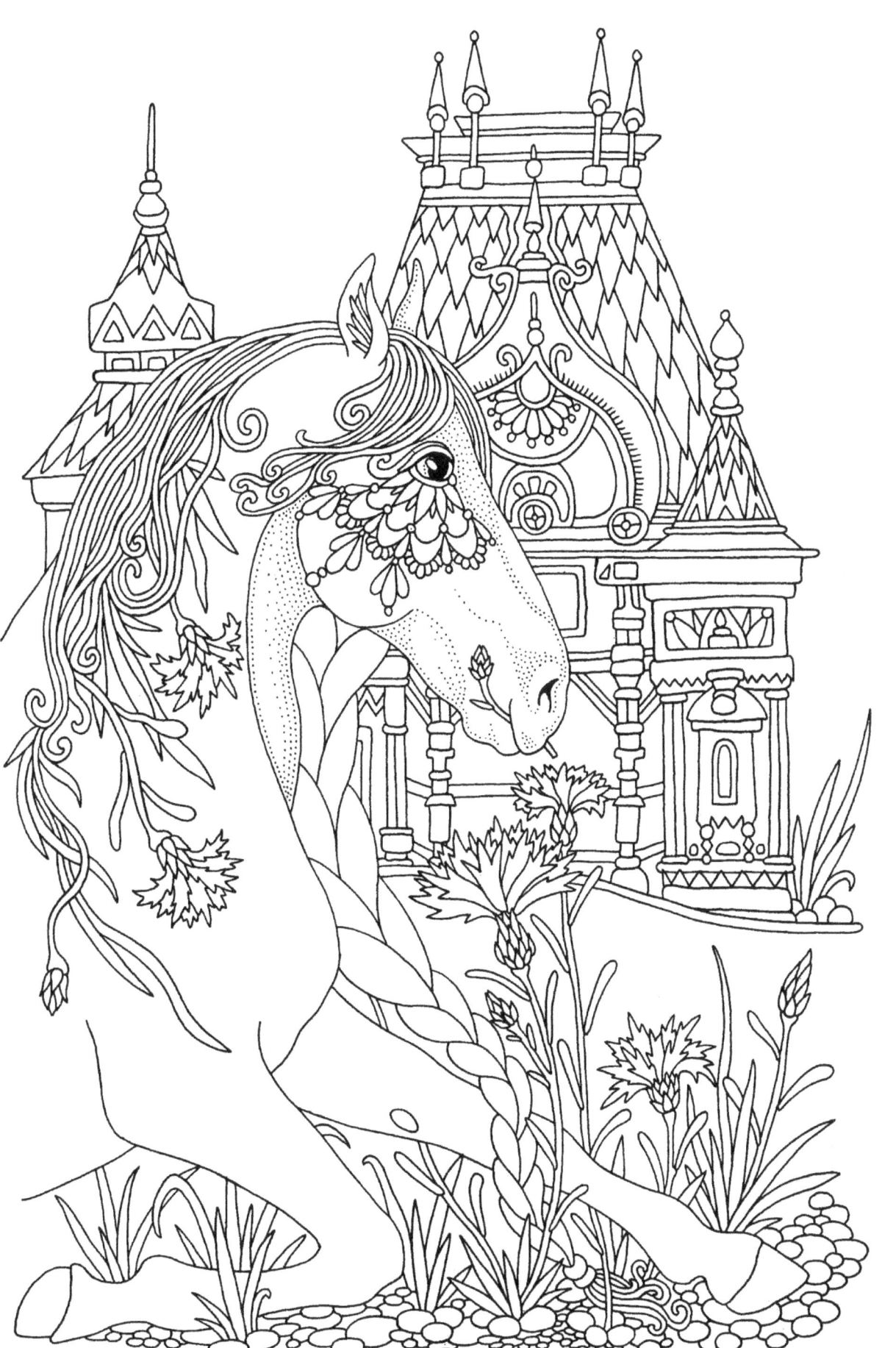

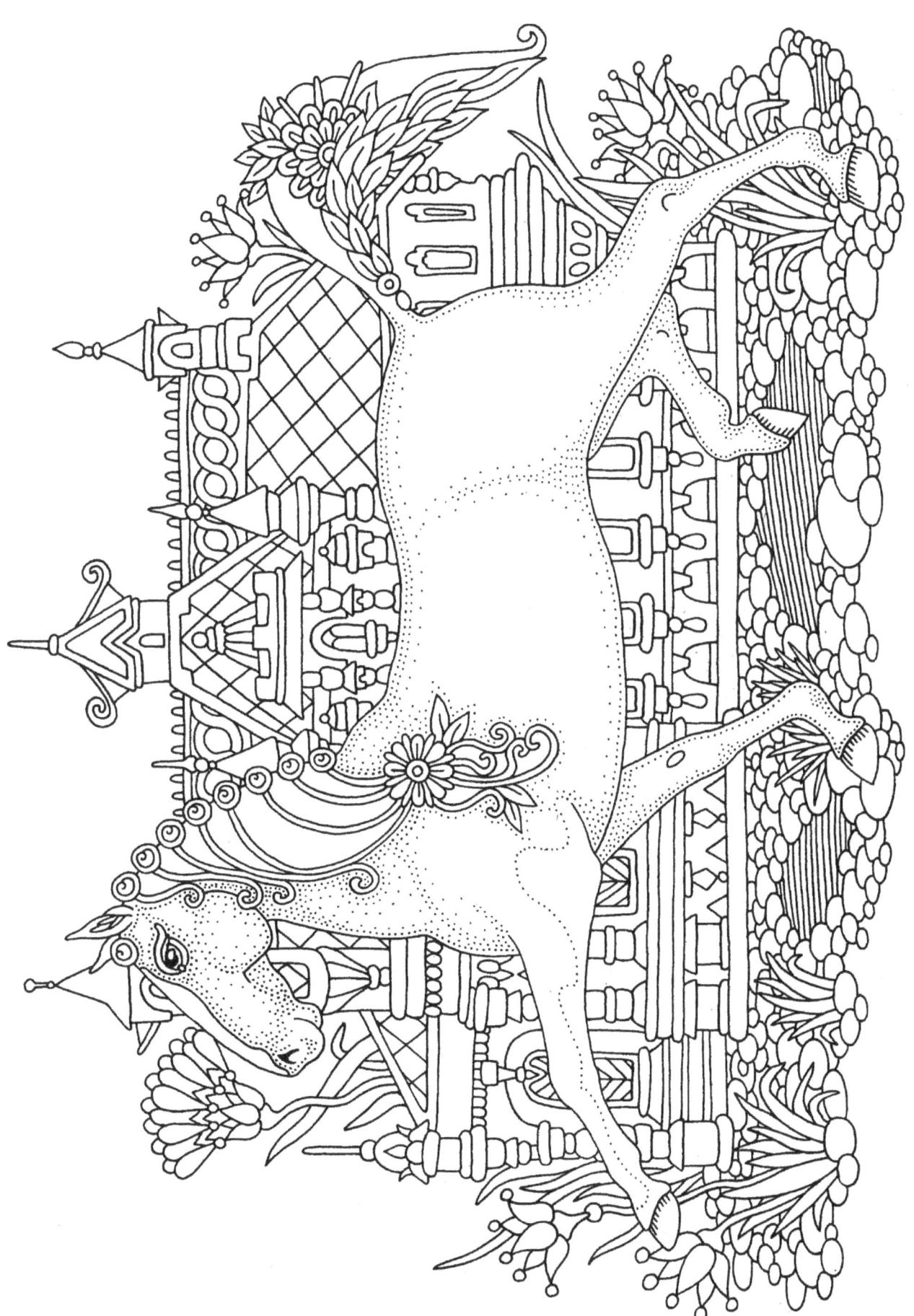

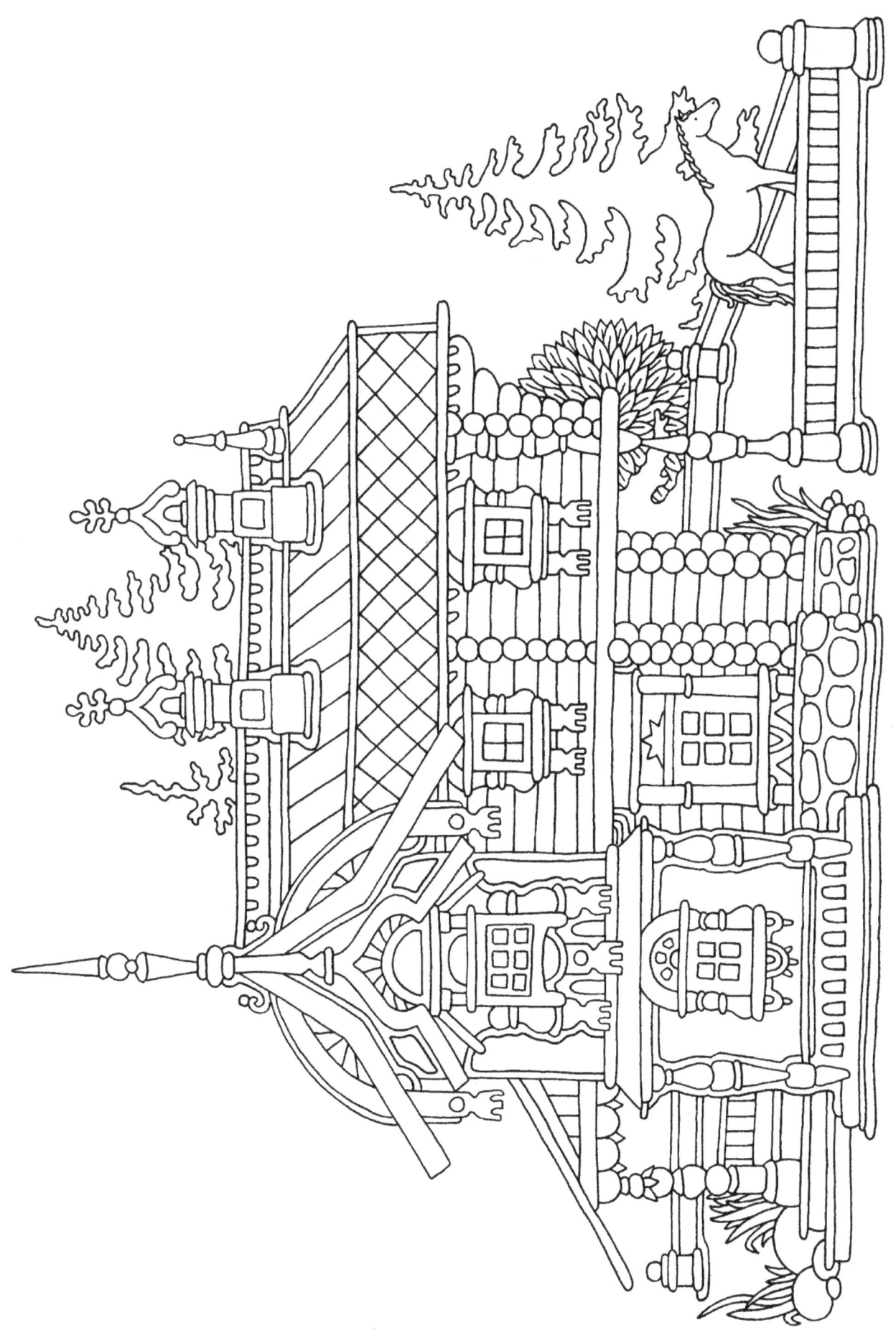

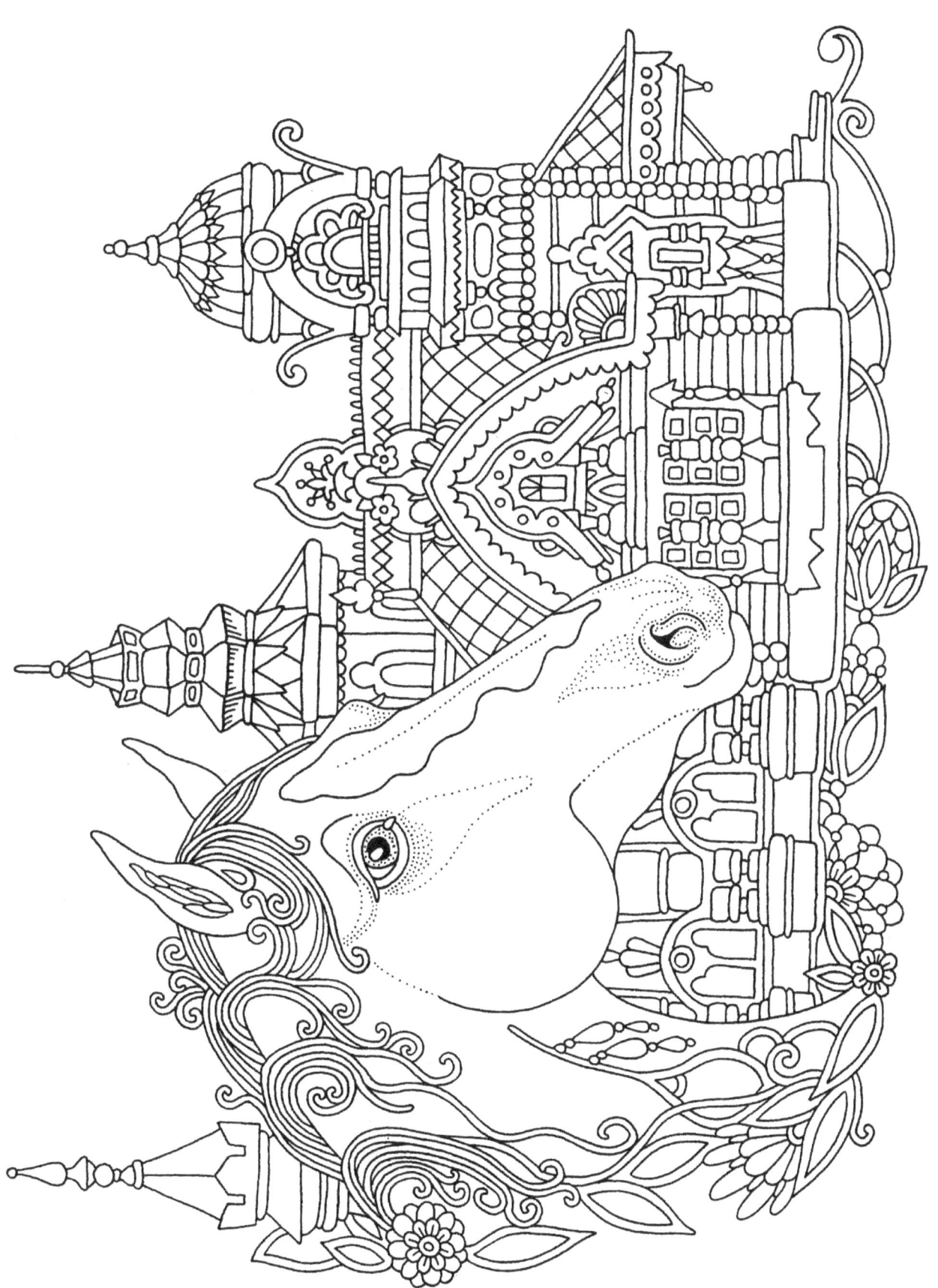

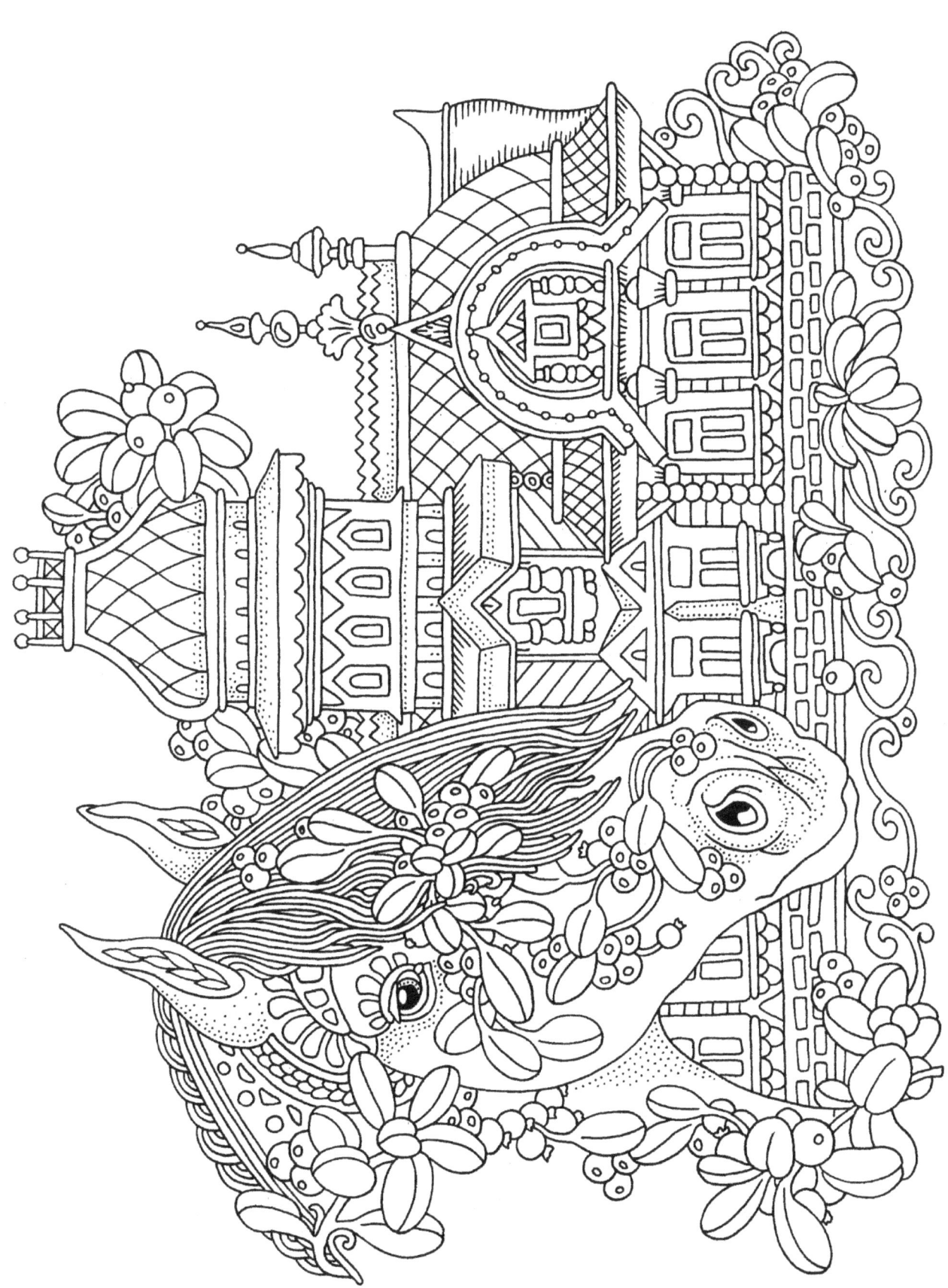

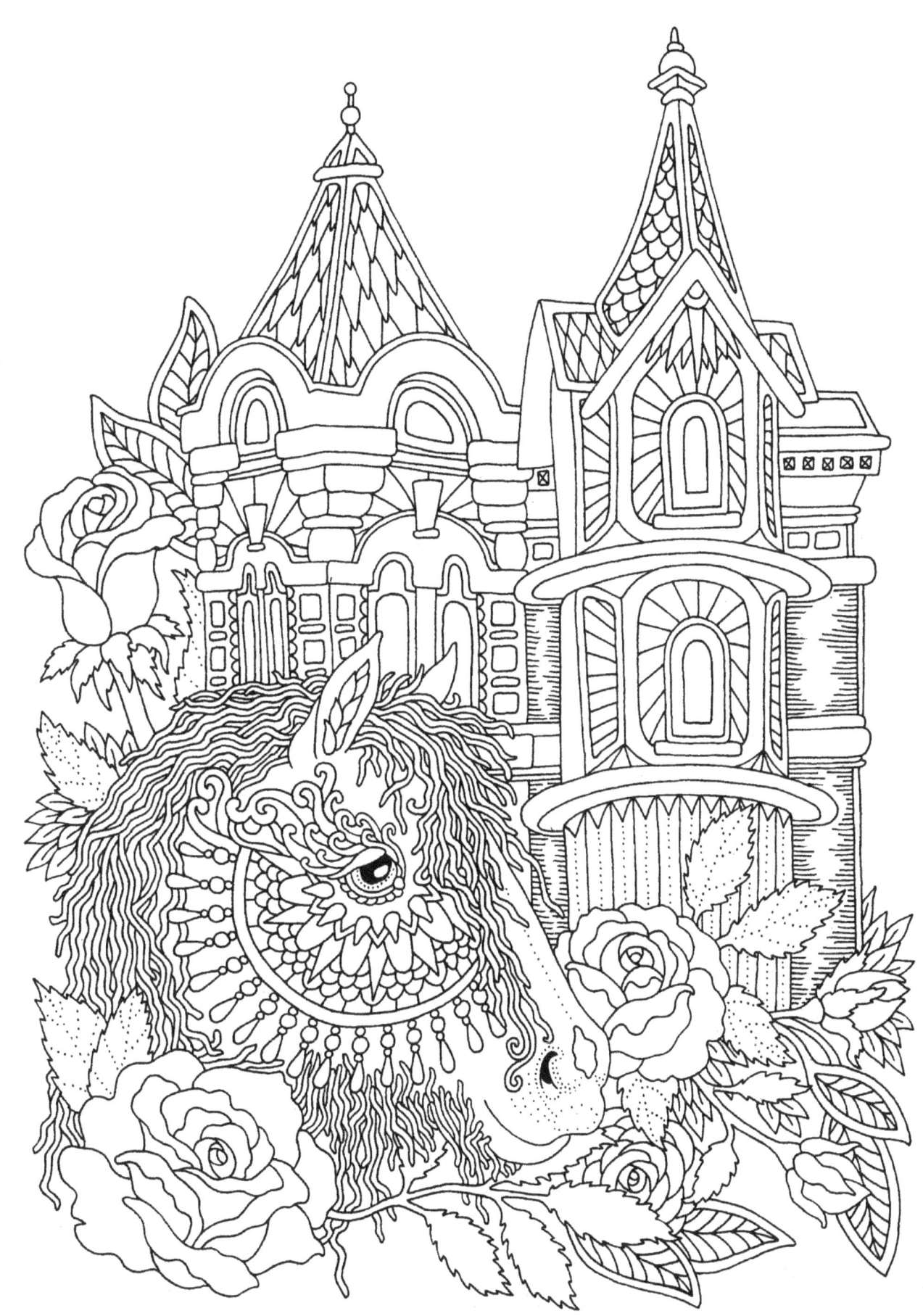

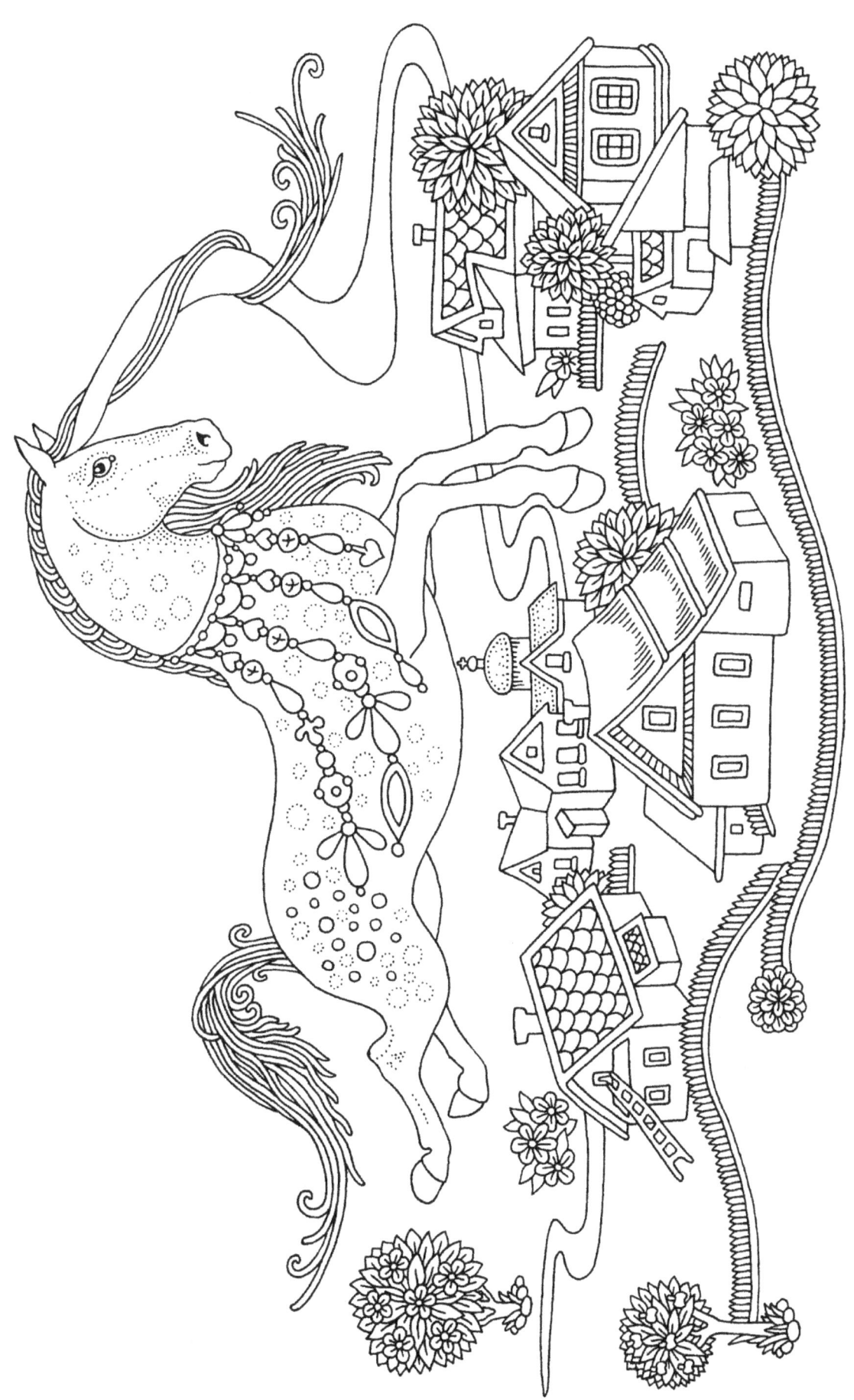

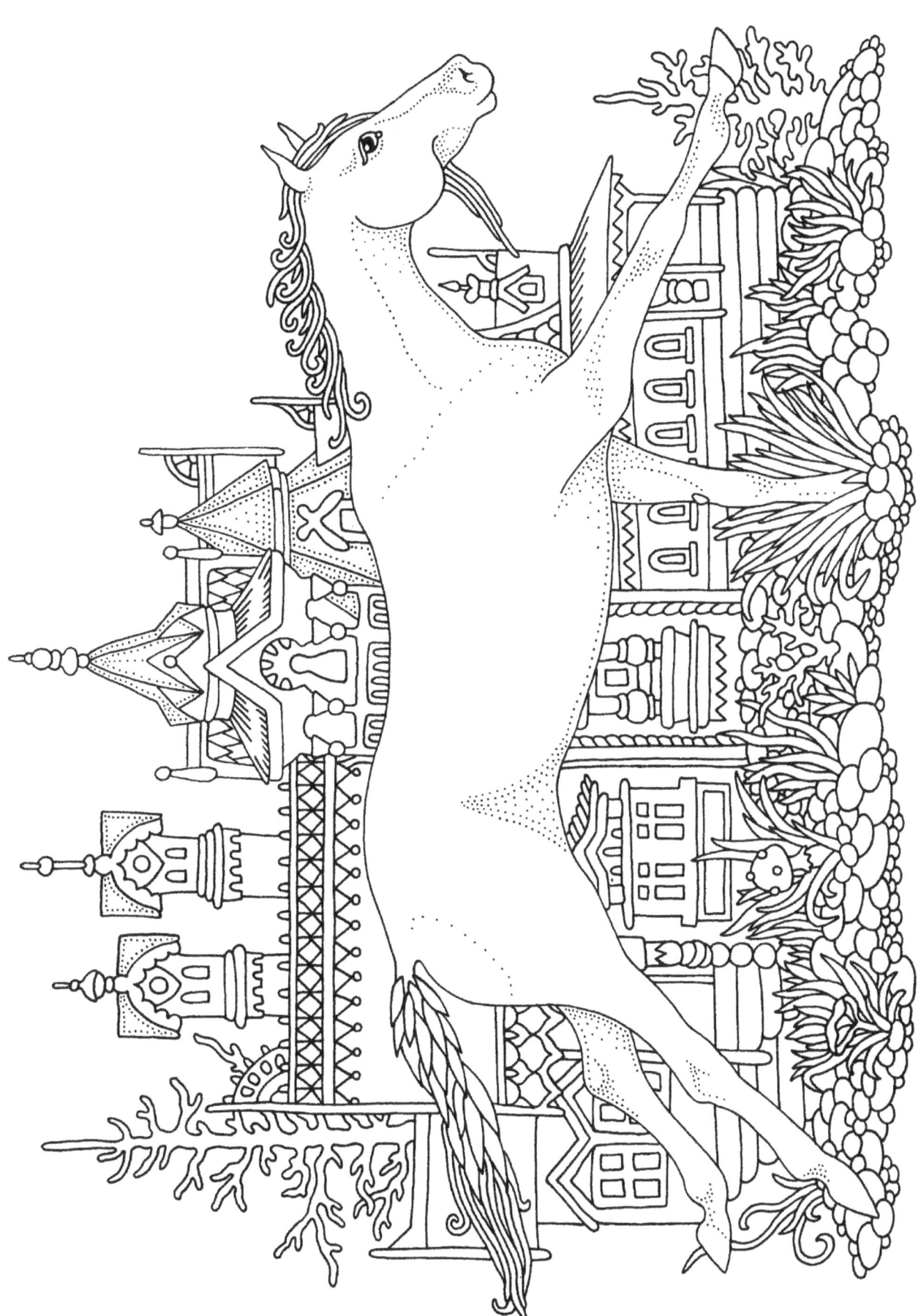

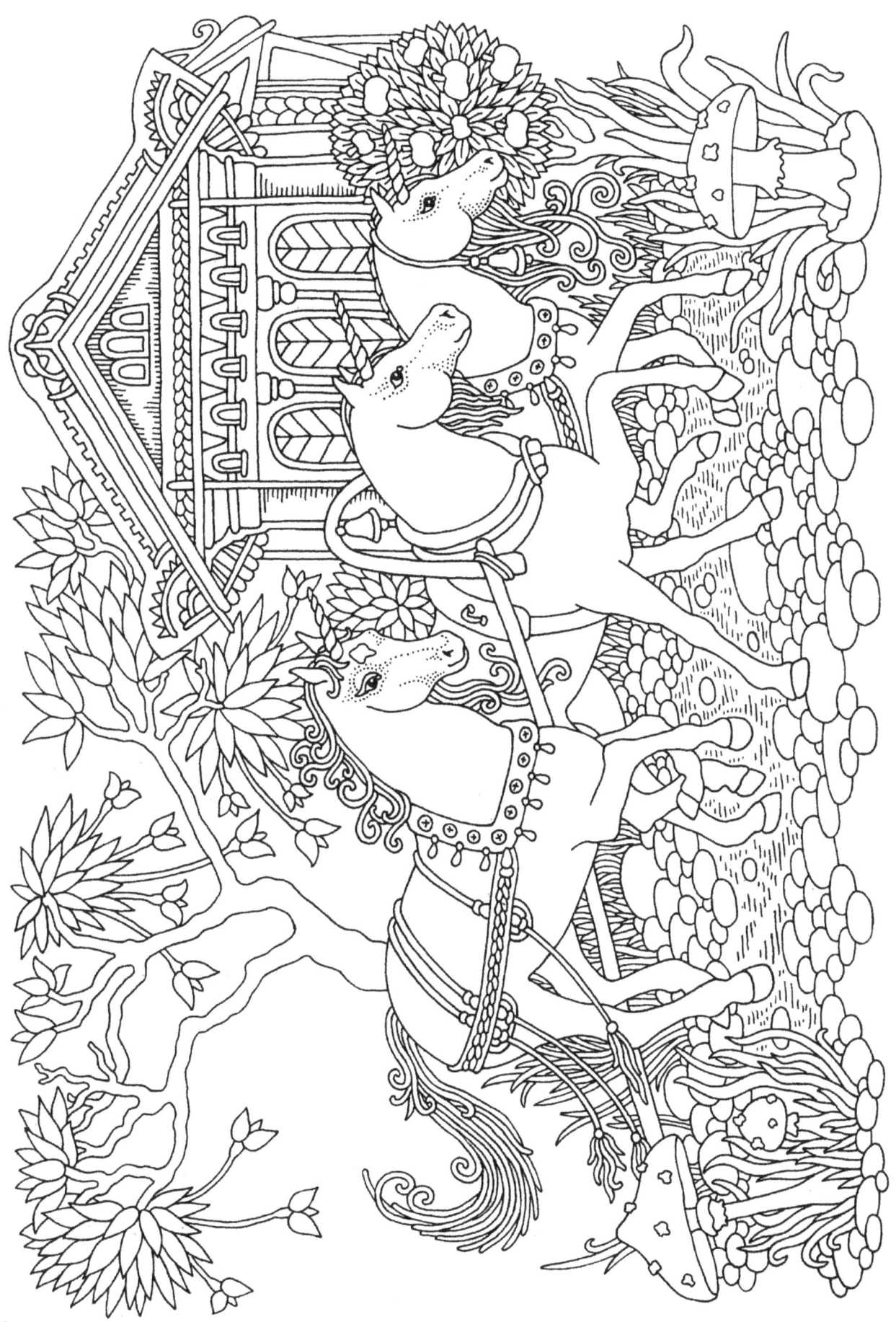

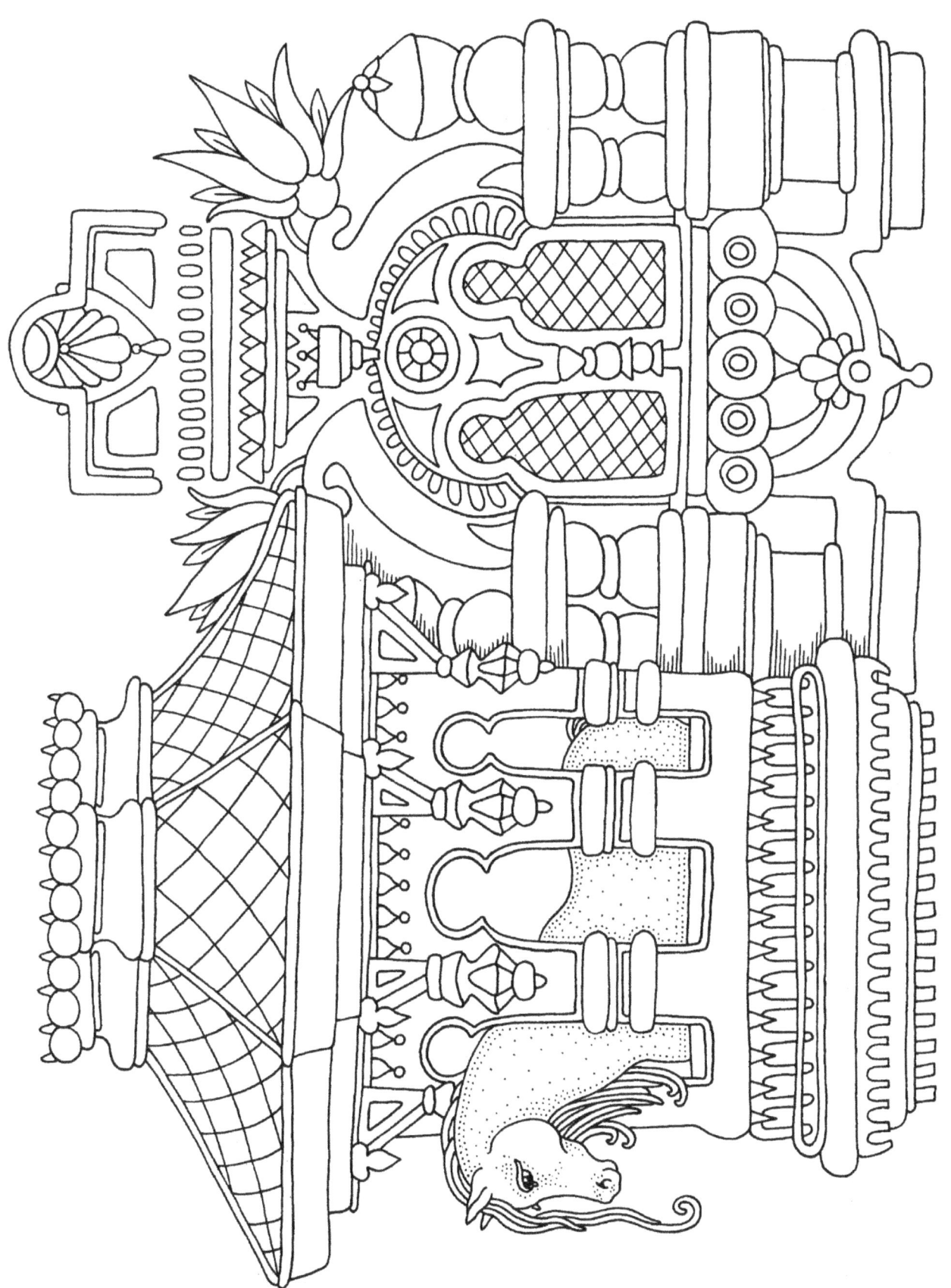

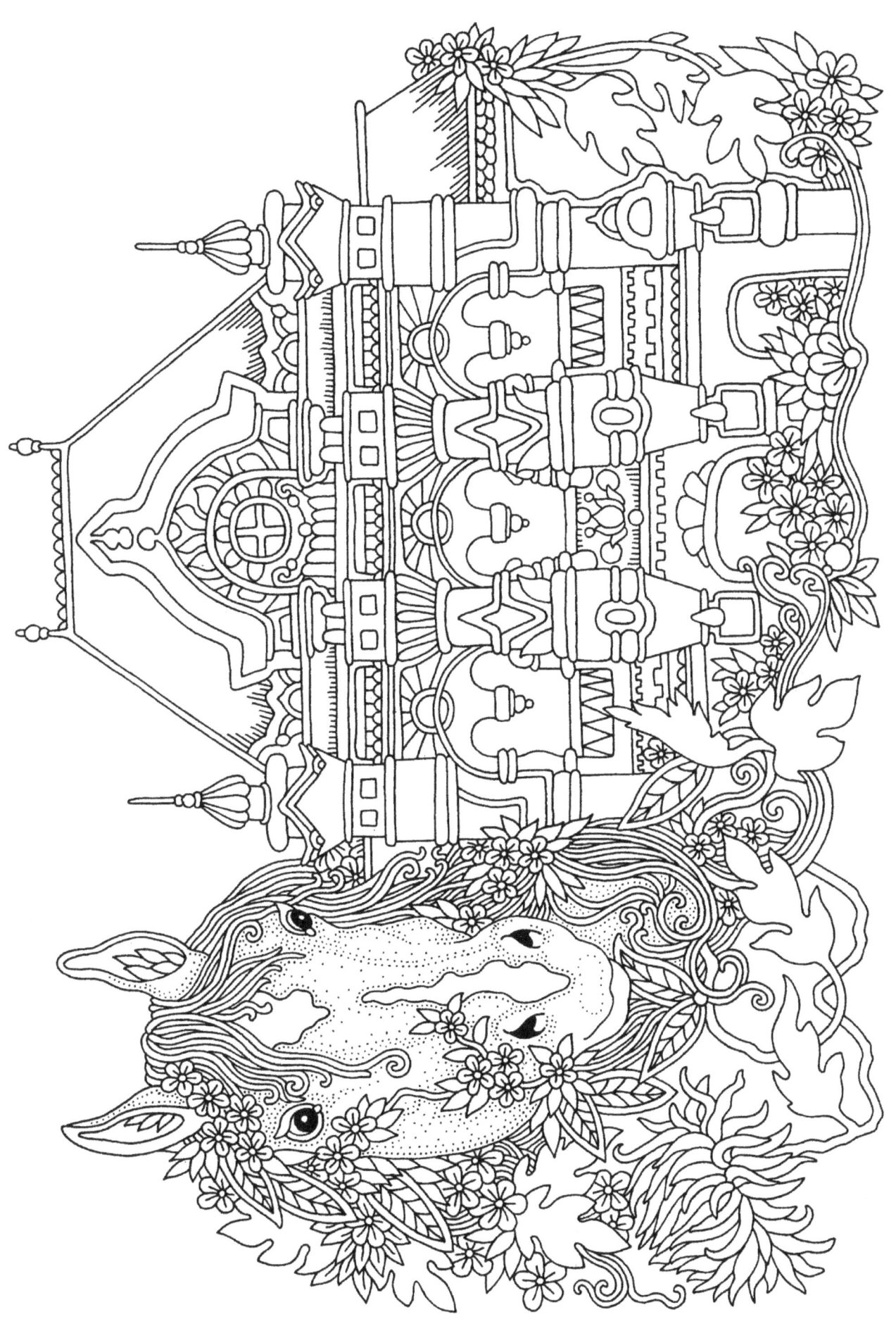

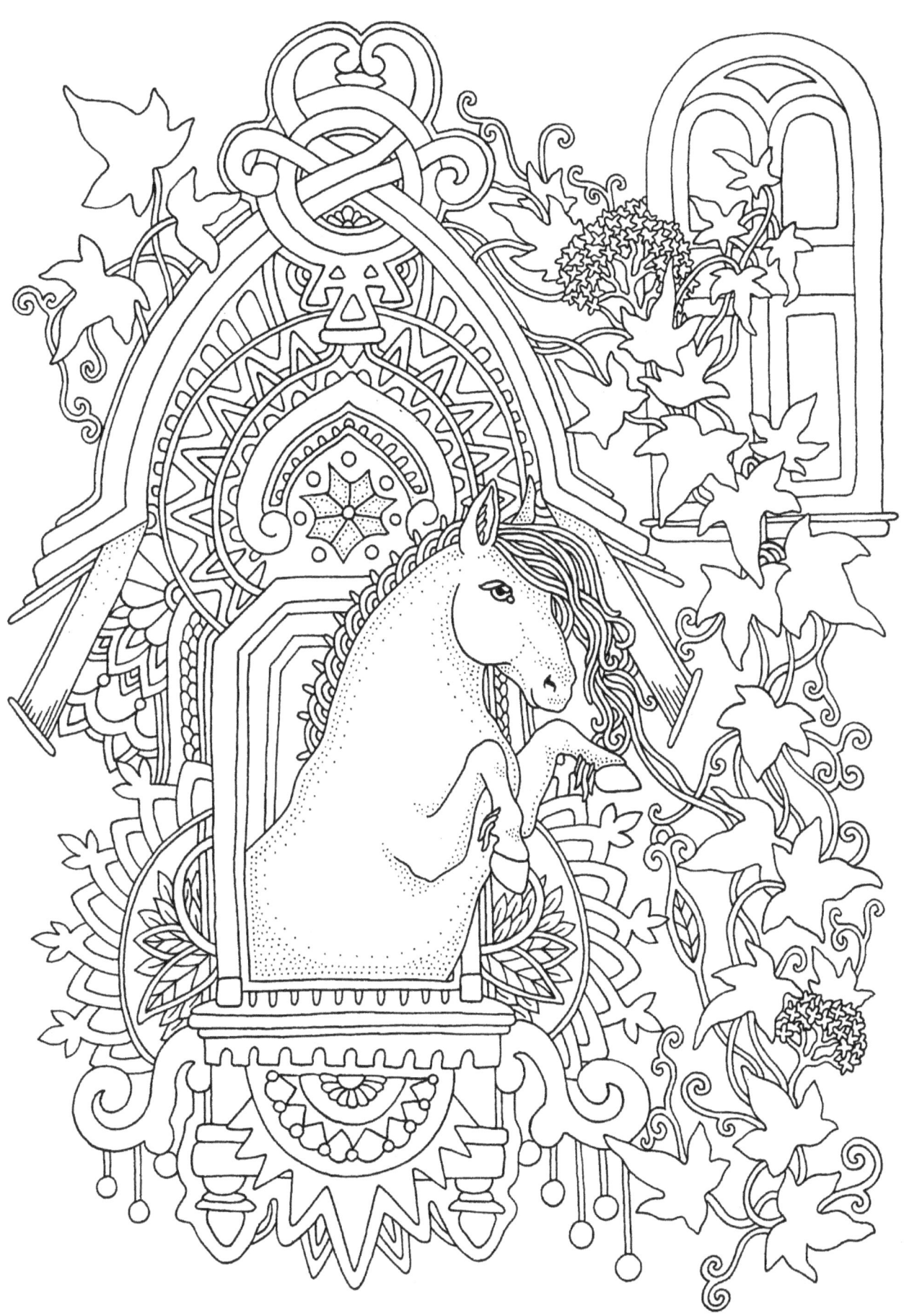

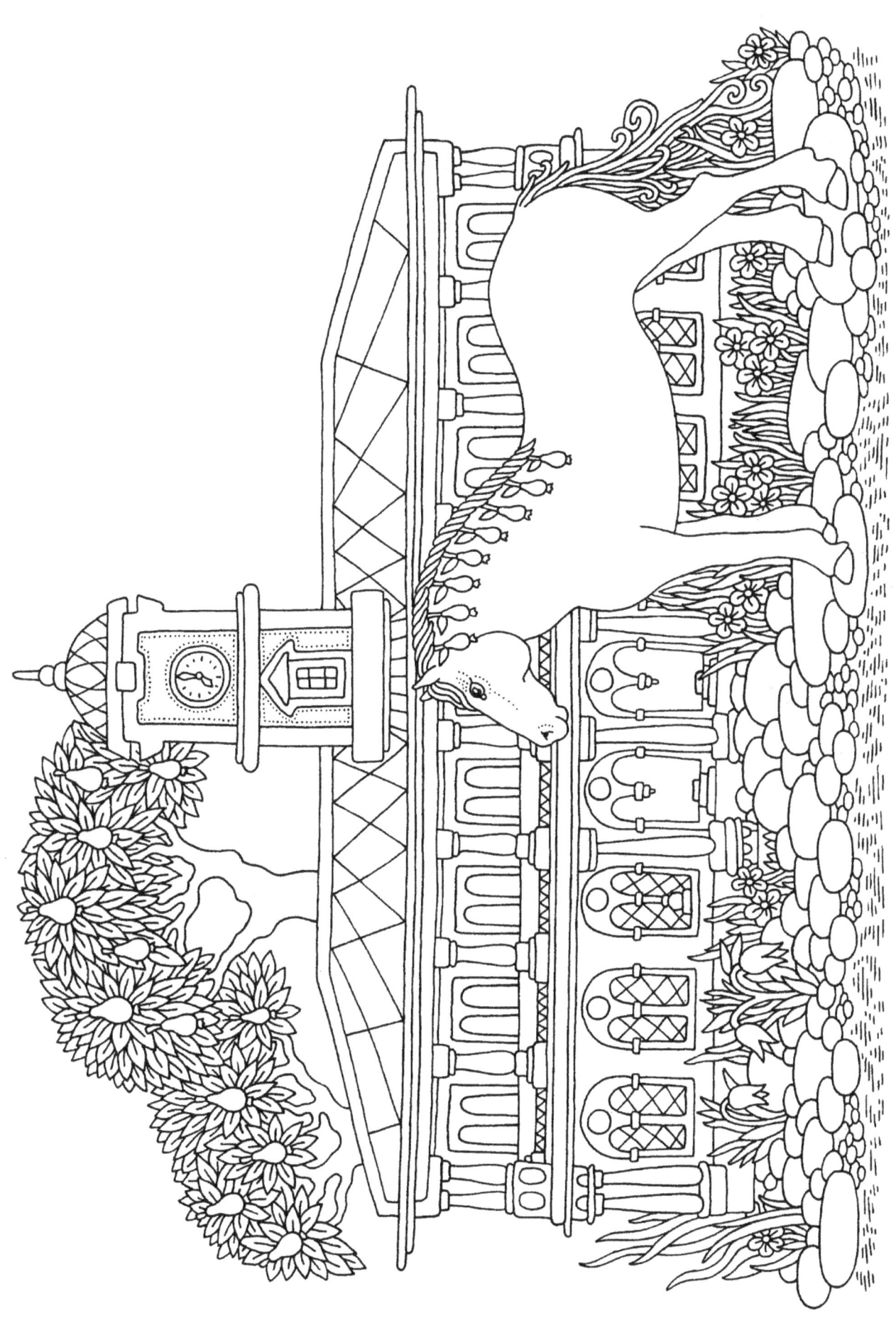

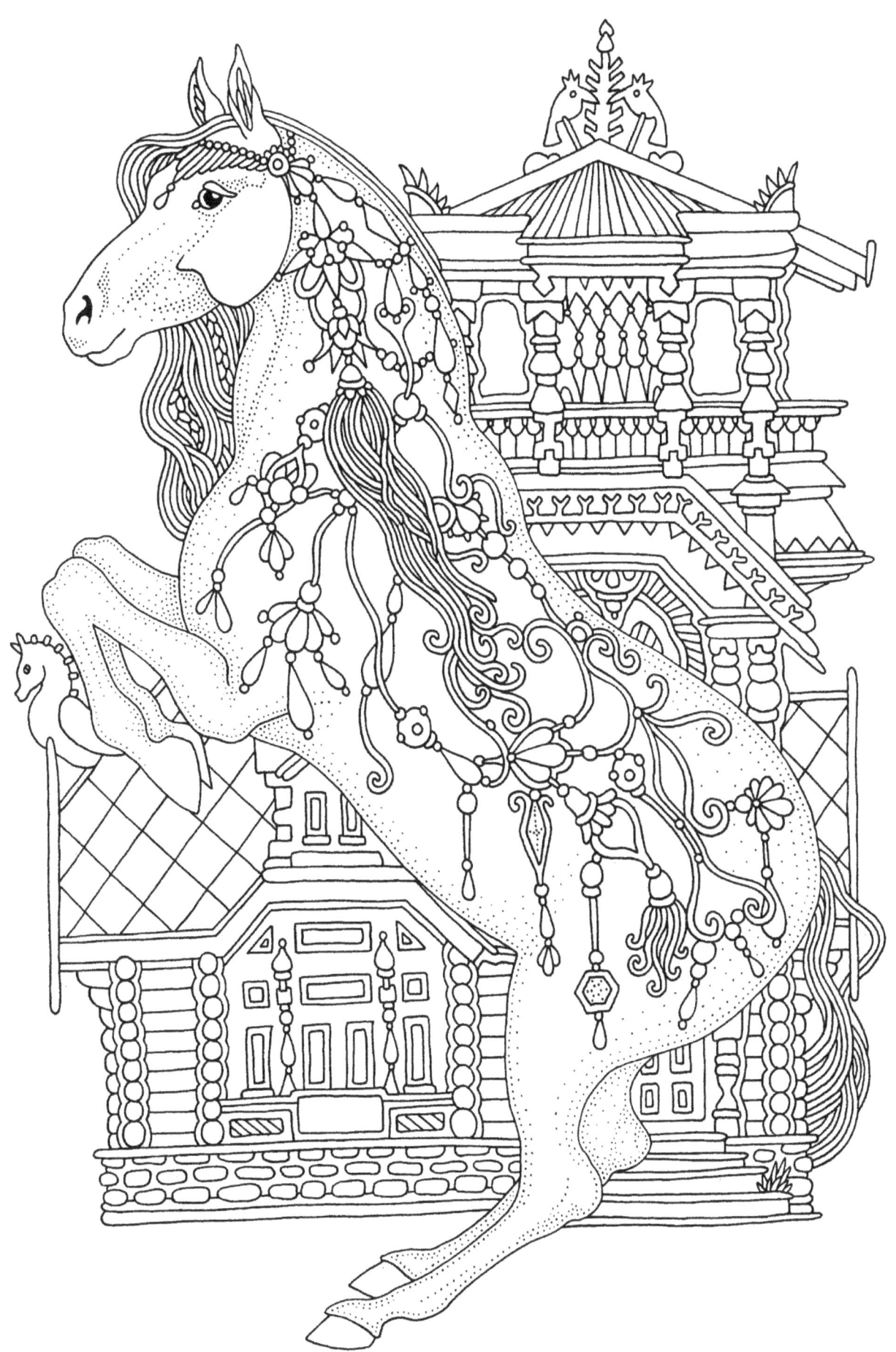

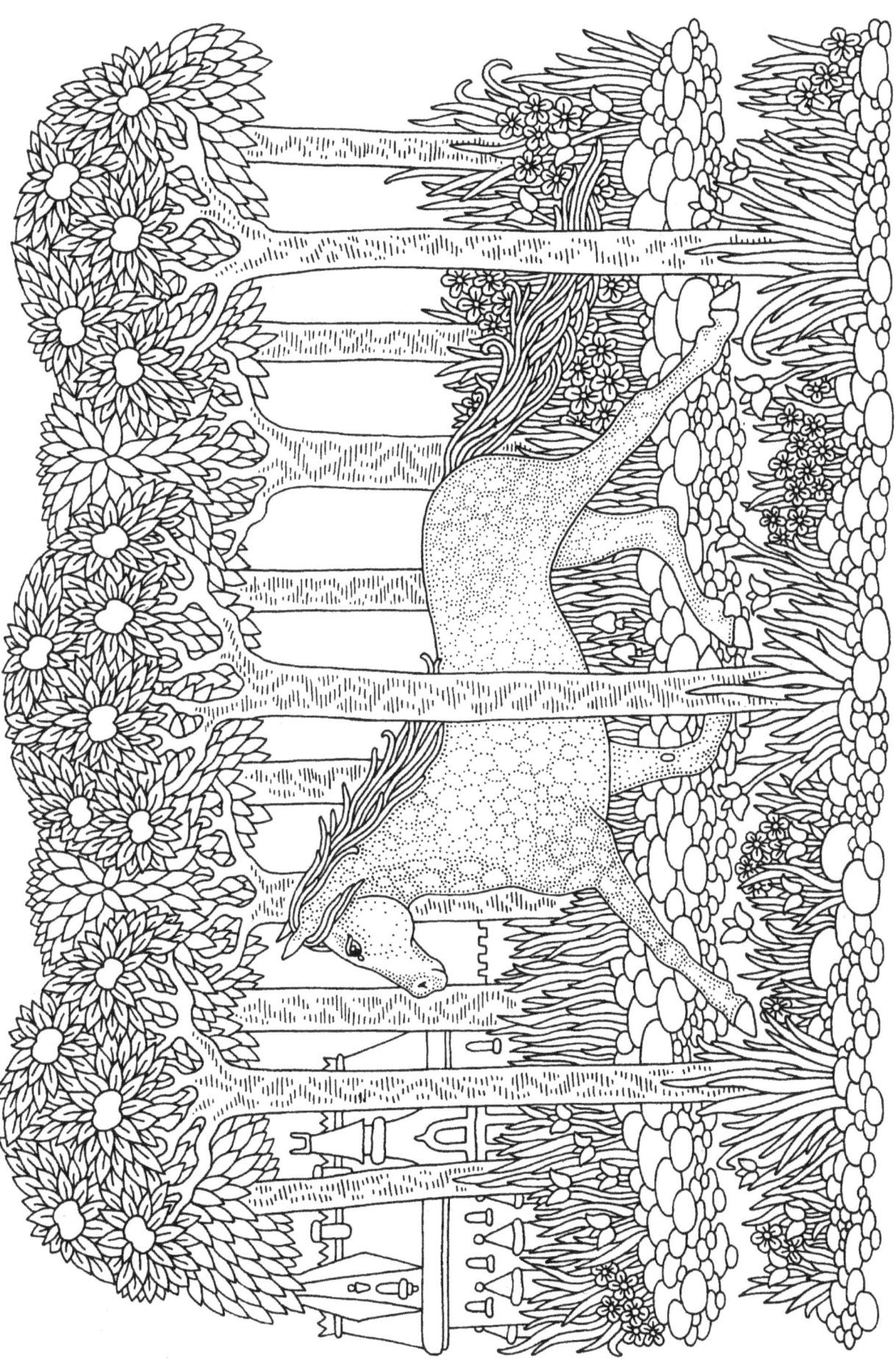

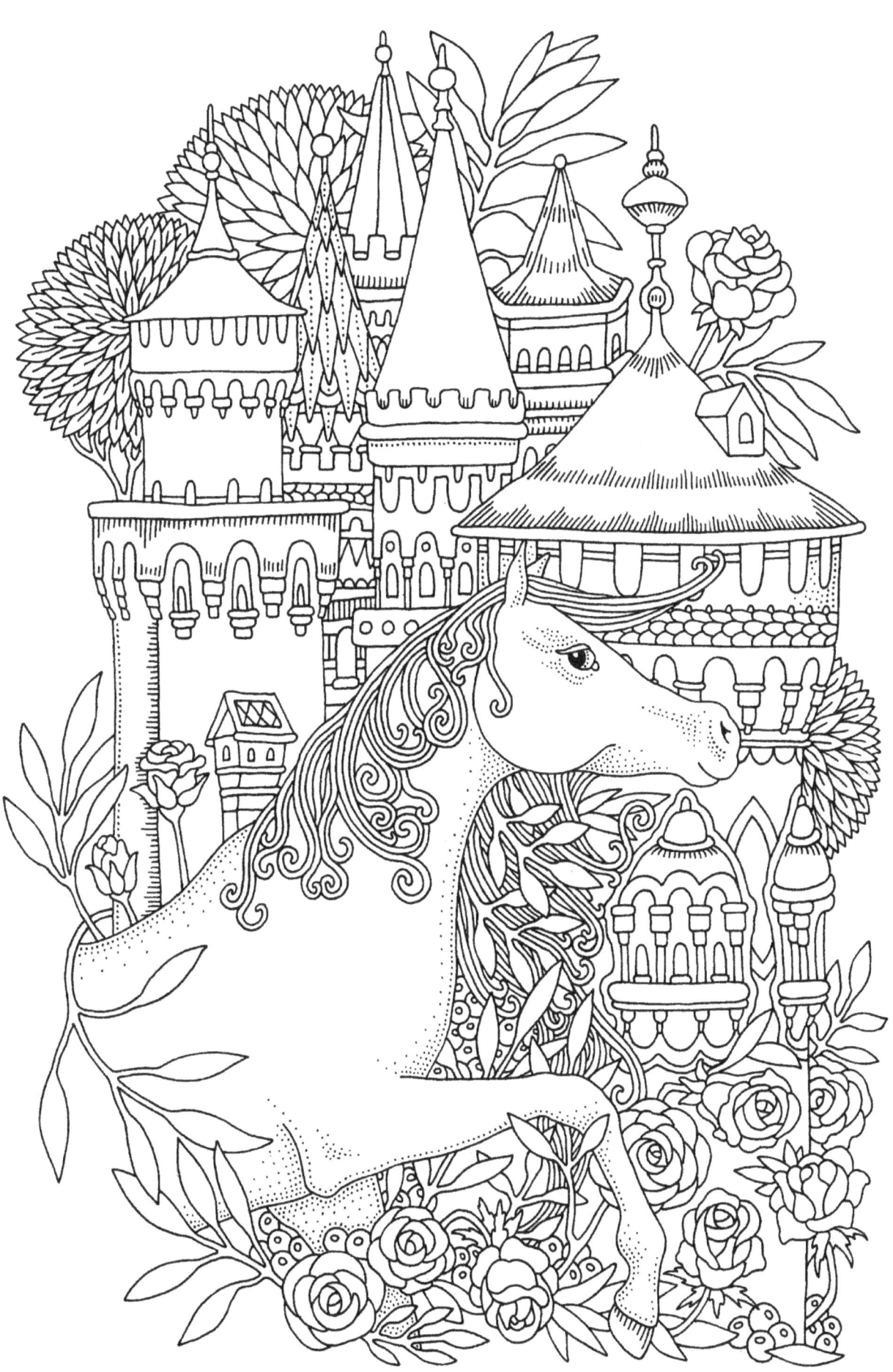

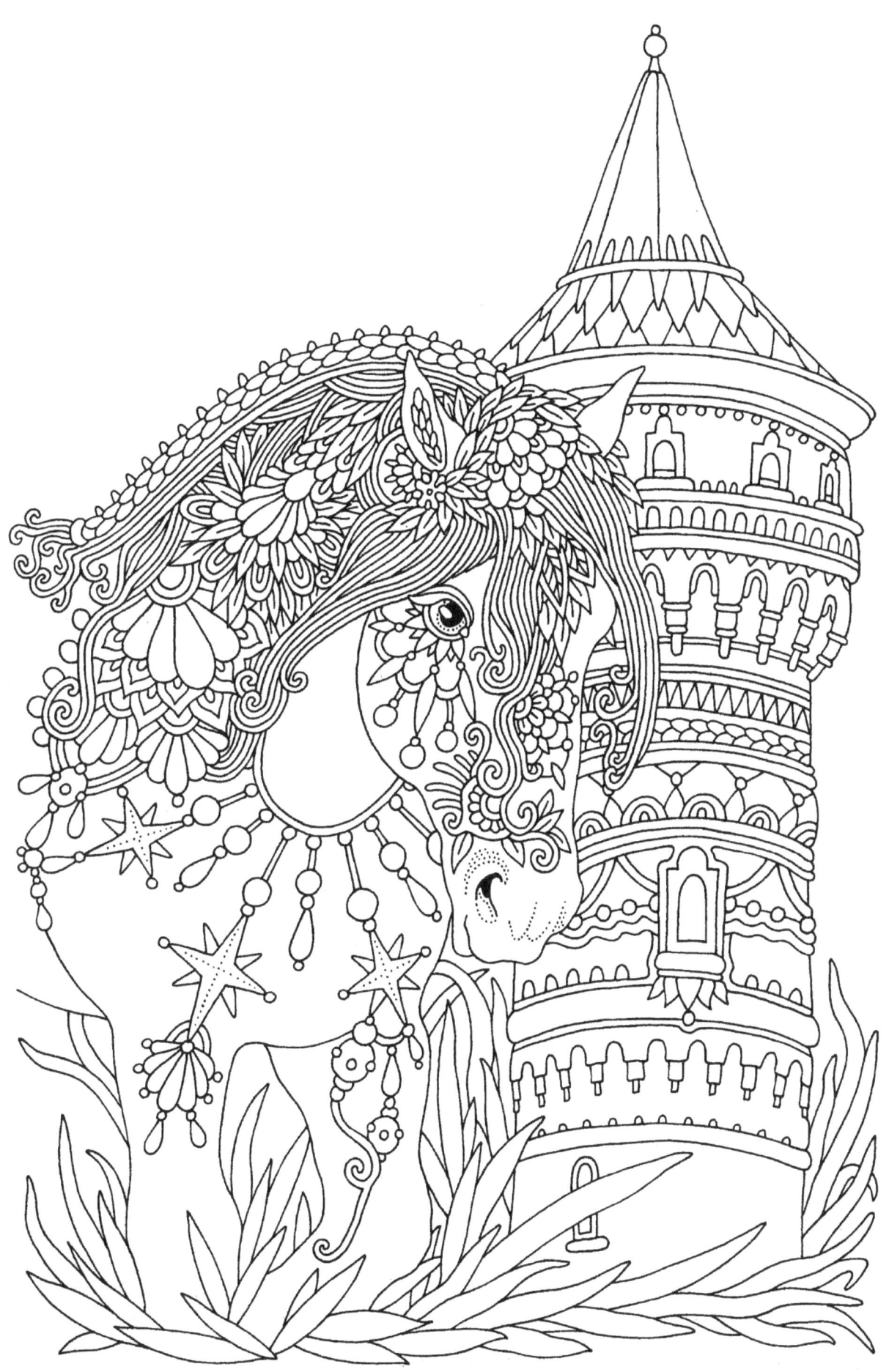

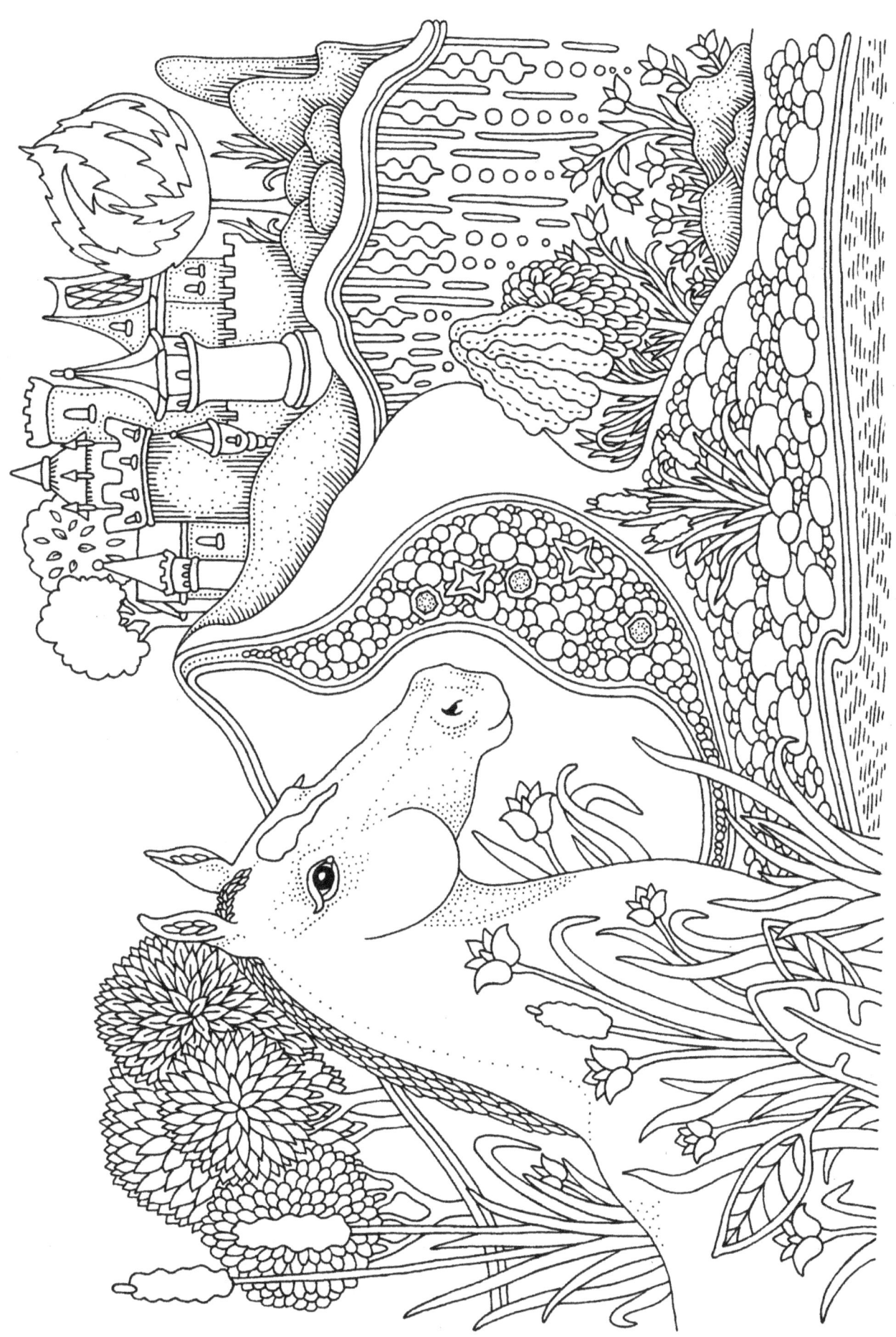

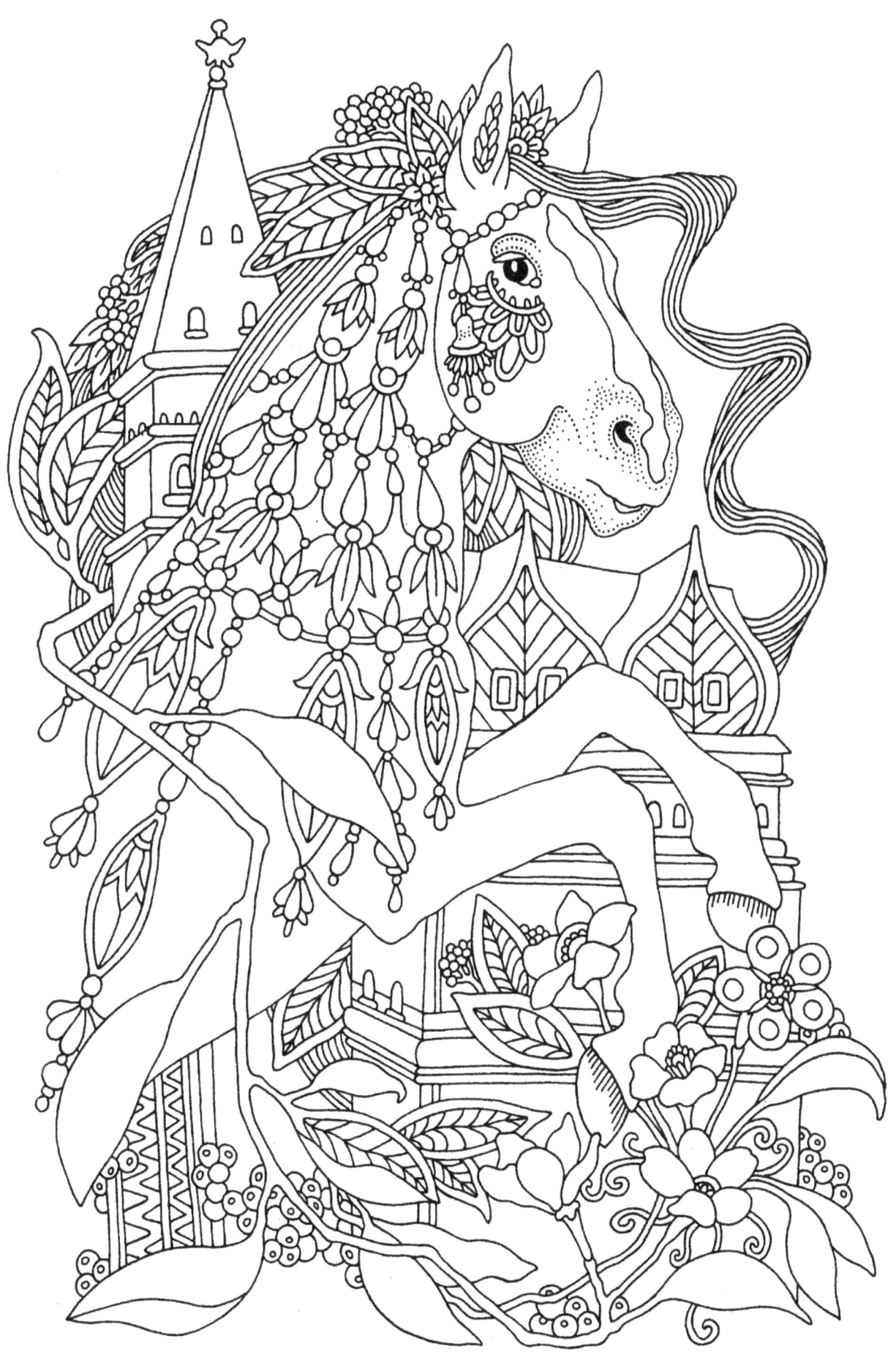

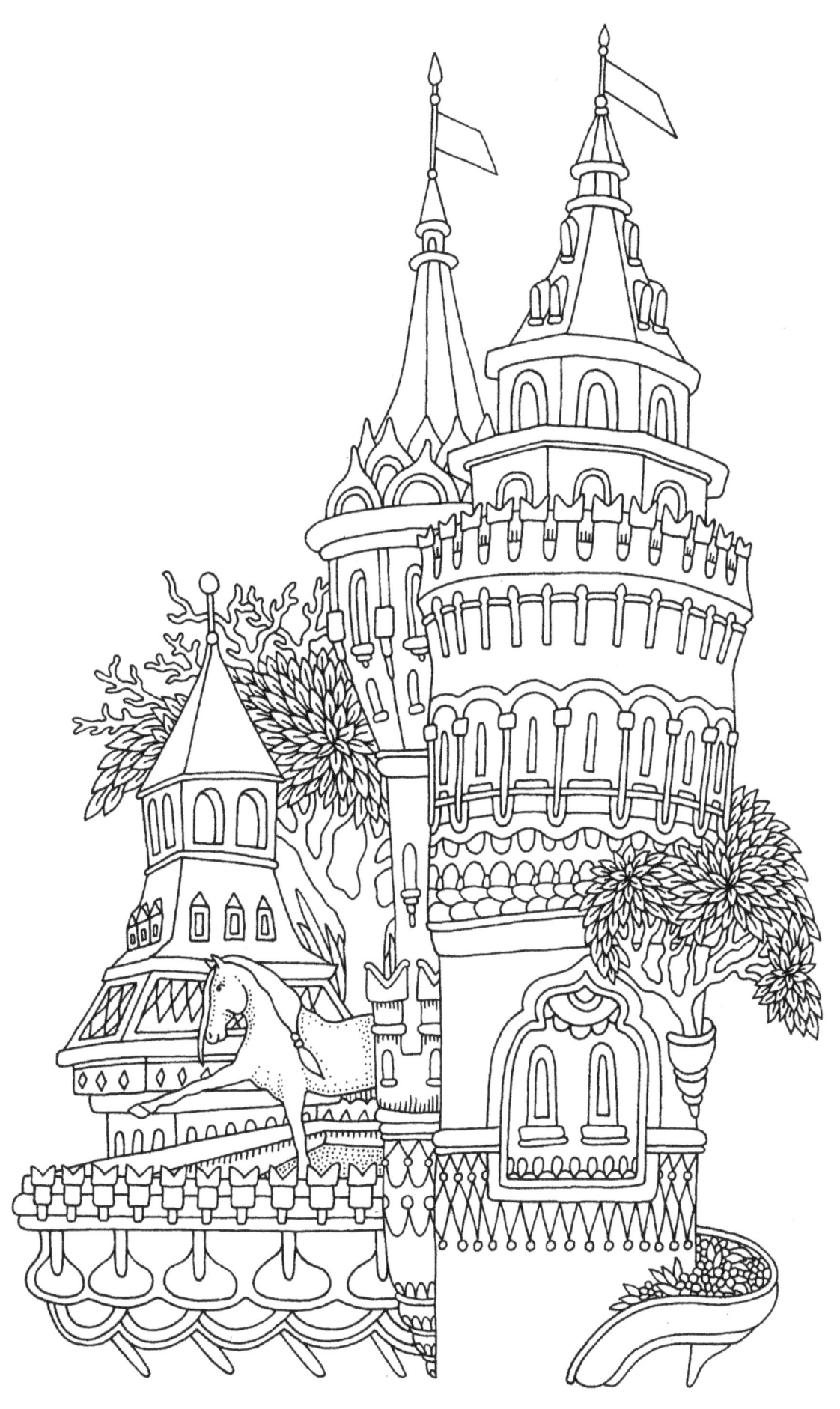

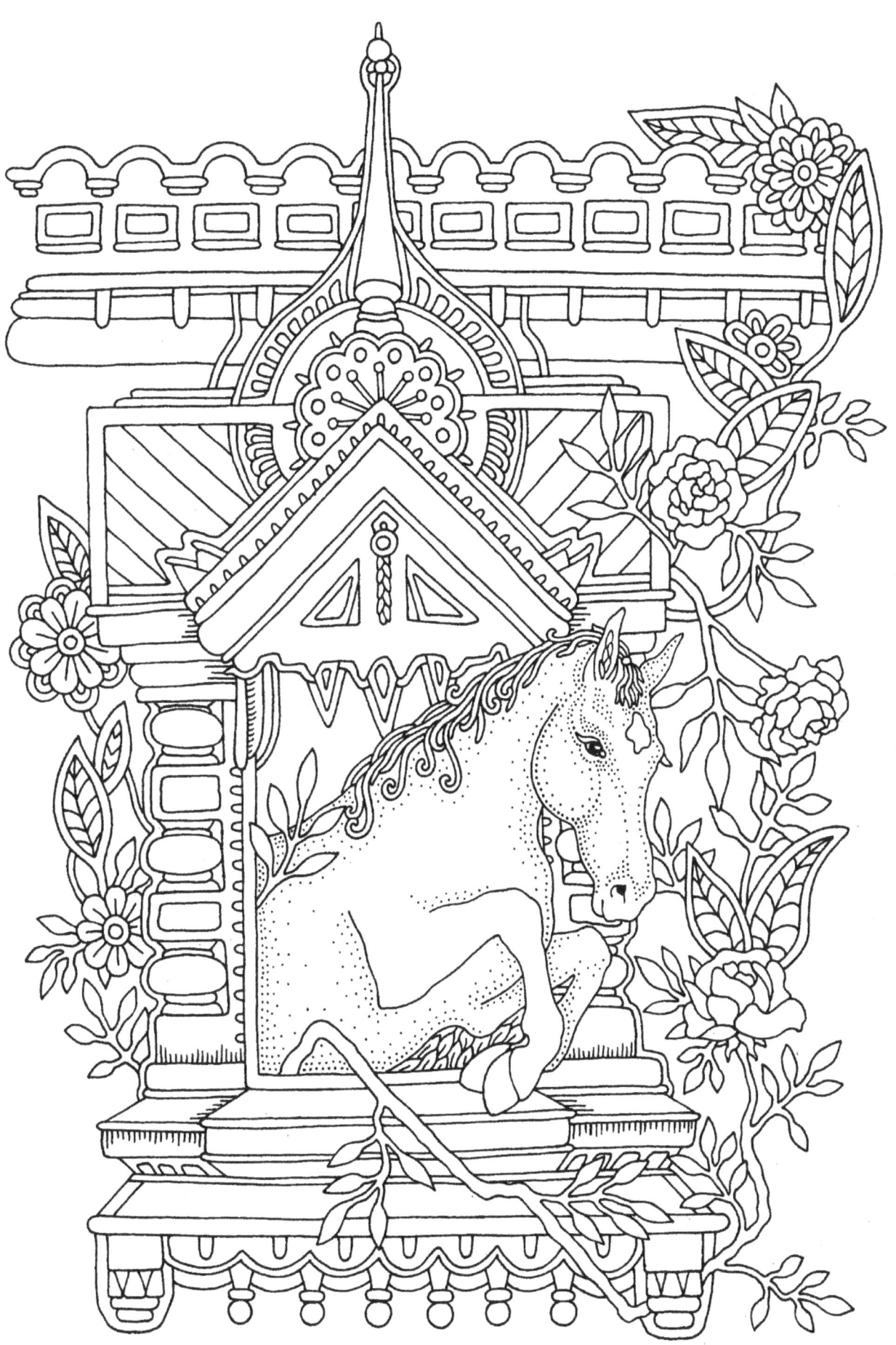

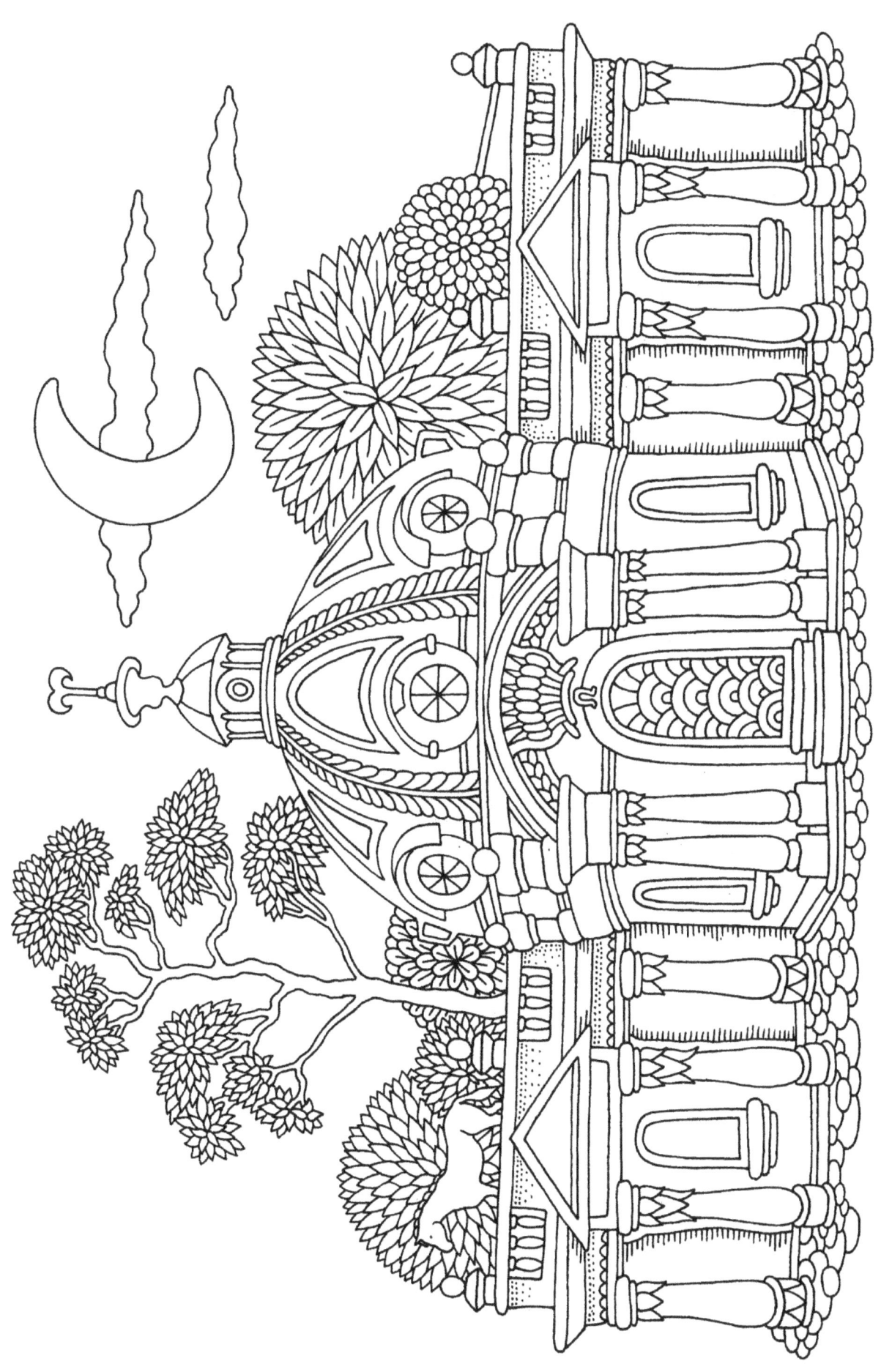